THE DETACHMENT PARADOX

*How an Objective Approach to Work
Can Lead to a Rich and Rewarding Life*

ANTHONY ZOLEZZI
WITH BILL BONVIE

ASM
BOOKS

For further information contact:

ASM Books
PO Box 3083
La Habra, CA 90631
Info@Detachmentparadox.com

Printed in Canada

Anthony Zolezzi with (Bill Bonvie)
The Detachment Paradox

1. Author   2. Title   3. Business
Library of Congress Control Number: 2004102936
ISBN: 0-9753157-0-6

To hard-working people that make a difference every day
—may they laugh, smile and thrive in any environment.

Acknowledgments

I'd first like to thank Linda Bonvie for her contributions to this project, including the cover design, Jennifer Todd for her work in editing this manuscript, and Joel Hochman, our publisher.

Special thanks go to my wife Lisa, my son Nicholas and daughter Alexis for living through 20 years of corporate ups and downs and entrepreneurial unknowns, and to my mom and dad for teaching me to stand up for my beliefs, no matter what, and never to compromise.

The greatest blessing an individual can have is a group of trusted friends and associates whom you can lay something like this book in front of and know they will give you honest, heartfelt feedback. Thanks so much to (in alphabetical order): Doug Aylesworth, Danny Bach, Rick Balsiger, Geoffrey Bloom, Patsy Beyers, Laura Coblentz, Susanne DeBoever, Clark Driftmeir, Dee Hock, Barclay Hope, Steve Horowitz, Kenny Lee, Tim Luberski, Myron Lyskanycz, Bill Nicholson, Pam Newton, Mike Oestreicher, Phil Reed, Mike Rempe, Mark Retzloff, Mark Sanano, Bill Shepard, Leah and Bob Stanek, Mike Tranchida, Dave Van Andel, Ed and Amy Summers, Larry Yee and Sol Zatt.

Table of Contents

Foreword

By Bill Nicholson

When I first read the exercises comprising this book, I couldn't help but be reminded of my experiences going through the Air Force's POW Training Camp.

As I watched the chaplain tear pages out of the Bible, while telling us "this is not your spirit, it is just paper and words," or had a gunny sack thrown over my head and a rope tied around my neck, it occurred to me that one of the keys to surviving months or years as a prisoner of war was the ability to detach—that is, to separate, and thus protect, one's inner and spiritual existence from whatever outside indignities and abuse one might be subject to.

Then it occurred to me that there is no similar training for entering the corporate world—no college courses to prepare graduates for a 25-to-30-year (or longer) period. No strategies for coping with the daily ordeal of being tied to a paycheck and benefits and beholden to a boss's orders, or for the various methods of fear and control that corporations exercise over their employees.

That, to me, is the real purpose of this book—as a sort of corporate P.O.W. (prisoner of work) training manual, one that can help you survive the experience with your values, identity and independent spirit intact. Whether you're a veteran corporate jobholder or just about to embark on your career, these exercises can guide you in the art of psychologically detaching from the control techniques that will be used on you, strengthening your inner resources and your ability to exchange information with fellow employees of the corporation, and to fortify your physical and mental defenses by identifying the humorous aspects of your situation and learning to laugh at them.

Best of all, it will help you to free yourself from the psychological control and emotional confines of corporate life, and become a happier, healthier and more productive individual.

Bill Nicholson has served as a Vietnam combat pilot, appointments secretary to former President Gerald Ford and chief operating officer of Amway Corp., and currently serves as vice chairman of Ideasphere Inc, Grand Rapids, Mich.

Introduction

If you saw the movie "Cast Away," you'll no doubt remember the character portrayed by Tom Hanks. He was the epitome of the company man—a hard-driven manager at Federal Express obsessed by timetables and a total dedication to the corporate mission. That is, until a fateful night when his plane is caught in a storm and goes down in the Pacific Ocean. He miraculously manages to survive, only to find himself stranded on a remote, uninhabited island where all of the artificial values and goals that had seemed of such utmost importance—his "corporate persona," so to speak—are rendered meaningless. Suddenly, he is faced with having to rely solely on his own inner resources.

Eventually, after many months of this Robinson Crusoe-type existence, he attempts a daring escape on a hand-made raft, is rescued, and returns home. Now, however, he is faced with a new challenge—that of read-justing to the world he left behind. And this time, he finds that his old identity, and all the priorities that went along with it, have lost their hold on him. Profoundly transformed by the experience, he has shed his corporate skin, and discovered his true sense of self, his true power.

The "discovery" of who we truly are is something that every one of us whose everyday existence is dominated by the need to get a paycheck, can achieve—maybe not in such a dramatic fashion, but to a degree sufficient enough to make our lives more satisfying, less stressful, and more fulfilling. The secret lies in separating your personal identity from your corporate one—that is, in being able to emotionally detach yourself from your job while holding onto whatever immediate security your paycheck provides.

The fundamental principle isn't all that complicated. When you realize that you are an individual with goals and objectives that your work has kept you from, you start looking at the job and the corporate structure objectively and without emotion. First, you must wake up to fact that control and fear factors are intrinsic to the very nature of corporations—particularly the stockholder-owned conglomerates that have come to dominate the contemporary scene. That is to say, without consciously doing so, the typical corporation begins to slowly control the people in its employ by unknowingly instilling a certain amount of fear that they may not get a check next week. This undercurrent of fear tends to permeate all levels of the organization, especially in any economic downturn, as reflected in such warnings as, "There will be layoffs if we don't make our numbers," or statements like, "In business, the only thing that matters is the bottom line." This is a subtle and slow process. In fact, most people don't realize it is going on. They are too concerned with the need for a regular paycheck and the fact that there are not that many places where they can get one—not to mention insurance, retirement and other benefits that weigh in.

Some ego-and-greed-based companies, however, control aggressively, operating without regard for the welfare of their employees. In one sense, these firms are easier to deal with, as there is no doubt about their agenda. These companies make no apologies for the uncivil treatment of employees who understand they are expendable.

Others companies make a point of eliminating bureaucracy and repressing the tendency to control their personnel, and may even gain reputations as enlightened employers. Such companies have a way of spawning incredible creativity and innovation in the process of achieving major aims and objectives. Unfortunately, even in these cases the pendulum often swings toward greater control in tough economic times. People who work for firms reputed to be "benevolent" start feeling increased pressure to devote more and more of their time and effort to the job. Such dedication may work for a while, but invariably the slow creep of fear and control can gradually overcome the individual. This leads to a steady erosion of the very employee attributes that are so essential to keeping a company successful—enthusiasm, creativity and innovation.

It is therefore essential to our well-being—and even to our ability to continue to be productive workers—that we separate our true selves, and wall off our emotional responses, from the companies for which we work. By that, I mean doing as good a job as you can for your employer while simultaneously working to strengthen your inner resources and aspects of your life that aren't job related. In other words, rebuilding and refocusing your true identity, so that even if the company you work for (or indeed, the entire corporate structure) were to simply vanish overnight, your own sense of self-worth would remain intact, as would your ability to survive and enjoy life. The Detachment Paradox, in essence, is the precept that employees who are managed by fear in a corporate structure will tend to be unproductive and unhealthy, whereas emotional detachment from the job, along with a sense of personal mission, can restore innovation and productivity at work and make for healthier and happier employees. The paradox here is that ultimately, by separating from the company emotionally, you actually become a more motivated employee. There's no question that when you are feeling good you're far more likely to put forth your best effort in anything you do.

It is not simply out of awareness of how expendable to the corporate structure even the most dedicated of us are that I make such a recommendation. It is also because your job, whether you're willing to admit it or not, has the ability to stealthily exercise control over your life, and without your realizing it, slowly suck you dry—and will continue to do so as long as you let it. The good news is you *do* have a choice. You have the choice to become a semi-conscious, stressed-out, unproductive employee or to manage yourself in a way that will enable you to be happier, healthier and more loving—all while maintaining the "company person" image and doing a great job to boot.

Unbeknownst to us (and unacknowledged in most corporations), the typical corporate structure uses many methods of command and control. The impact this can have on employees' lives is profound. According to Dr, Paul Rosch, president of the American Institute of Stress (AIS), an estimated 1 million workers are now absent daily due to stress, costing American industry $300 billion a year in terms of diminished productivity. What I've observed, however, is that employees themselves often don't realize just how stressed out they are, and it may take a spouse or significant other to recognize the toll that unrelenting job pressure is taking not only on yourself but on your relationship.

Amazingly, you have the choice to dispense with most of this stress, and thus to be more productive and creative in your job. Over a quarter century ago, I went to work for a major Fortune 200 company. I spent ten years in that environment, becoming intimately familiar with its inner workings as a member of the management advisory board to the board of directors and as a company "fast track" participant. But despite having what was considered a key role in the corporate growth pattern, I felt increasingly uncomfortable and out of my element. (For one thing, being from southern California and not the Midwest, I never quite adapted to the idea of having to put on a jacket every time I went to the cafeteria.)

This was where I first started to learn about emotionally "detaching" from my company job—of psychologically distancing myself from my surroundings and pressures. At first, I probably did so as a kind of natural defense mechanism, without quite realizing what it meant—but when it occurred, I soon discovered that my perceptions of what was going on around me had sharpened considerably. The phenomenon that I found to be most interesting was that the more I emotionally detached, the clearer my thought processes became, and the more productive I was. And in the end more people wanted to work with me because somehow without altering my environment I had learned how to view it from a different perspective, without the emotional involvement that had slowly been turning me into a sleepless wreck with bags under my eyes. The calm and positive attitude I exuded was becoming contagious. I began to realize and observe how unhealthy an environment this corporation was for those involved. Despite all the economic benefits their positions afforded, some of the company's highest ranking officers seemed to be in the worst shape of all, chain-smoking cigarettes, downing endless cups of coffee, getting little or no exercise, and generally putting themselves on a fast track toward a heart attack and a host of other medical problems.

Might all this add up to a pattern of gradual self-destruction? I wasn't sure, but it was something I was determined to avoid at all costs, and I knew it could be sidestepped with the right perspective. Remember, I wasn't yet completely aware of the change that had come over me, but in a way it was as odd and paradoxical as one of those old episodes of the Twilight Zone. Here I had managed to break free in an emotional sense from the invisible bonds of fear and control. I was smiling more and laughing at issues that would have panicked me a month before. In meetings I was so objective and "cool" that instead of raising eyebrows, I was making better decisions and getting more kudos from top management. The funny thing was, however, that it really no longer mattered that much to me. Since my original intent had been to devote no more than ten years of my life to this particular company, I now felt more equipped than ever to go through with that plan. (Don't get me wrong—after ten years, there were many people that I liked working with, so the decision to leave was not nearly as cut and dried as it appears here.)

On the 10th anniversary of my joining the company, I announced to the group I was leaving—in fact, leaving St. Louis, where the company was based, and, at the urging of my wife Lisa, moving back to the West Coast. Everyone naturally assumed that I had gotten a better job offer—but I hadn't. Instead, I had accepted an opportunity to be part of a leveraged buyout that I wasn't sure would ever materialize. My goal was to discover who I really was and what I was capable of achieving on my own. I had come to the conclusion that something about the corporate pyramid of command and control from the top down wasn't a structure that worked for me. And I have since concluded that it doesn't really work for millions of other employees, either—although they might not be as inclined to take a risk as I was, particularly in uncertain economic times. That, in fact, is precisely why I set about writing this book—to help those millions of workers cast off the psychological chains of the corporation without having to leave their jobs or risk losing a regular paycheck.

Since leaving my former company, I have gone on to build several businesses based on different types of organizational models that I have made a point of studying. Throughout my career, I have had the experience of serving as a consultant to a typical, publicly-owned "command-and-control" company while simultaneously creating from scratch bold new enterprises involving innovative ideas, fast-paced execution and a "change-the-world" outlook. The contrast is truly amazing— the difference between a strictly "for-profit" operation whose actions are based on a risk-averse philosophy or the effect something will have on quarterly earnings and a dynamic one where values such as trust reign supreme.

Most of my career has been spent in the "risk-averse" manage-by-fear corporate environment. What I have learned, after having expended an inordinate amount of time in fighting this particular fear-driven windmill, is the futility of trying to produce significant change in a corporate culture. Business may undergo radical transformation in technology— as, for example, where we are today in terms of instant worldwide communications as opposed to twenty years ago when even fax machines were few and far between. But the basic structure of the corporation, which originally evolved centuries ago in Medieval Europe, has continued to remain static—with power emanating from a supreme head and a 3,000-year-old hierarchical system designed to operate without emotion, to compel and manipulate, to discourage individuality, initiative and innovation, and to discard people like so many disposable pieces of equipment when their services are no longer desired. Those may sound like harsh words coming from as positively oriented a person as myself, but I want to get your attention. This is the structure we have inherited, and you need to be aware of what's embedded in the corporate DNA. Did you ever wonder where common business phrases like "you are not paid to think" or "it's my way or the highway" came from? During tough economic times even notable corporate exceptions are eventually apt to be whipped into conformity, giving in to irresistible forces such as consolidation and shareholder demand for immediate gain that are almost certain to compromise the best of intentions. The irony is that enthusiastic and innovative employees are exactly what's needed at such times to find ways of turning things around. But a corporation, with all its boxes and individual fiefdoms, has trouble recognizing that fact.

Where we can bring about change however, is in ourselves, and the ways in which we respond to the people and the corporate strategies that are unconsciously starting to control and coerce us through fear. The thing you must keep uppermost in mind is that *once you stop responding emotionally to such tactics, the corporation has lost its control over you.* By emotionally detaching, you regain personal power. Perhaps that's how we can influence the course of corporate events, and start to be treated like human beings instead of replaceable parts of some huge, impersonal machine—by enough of us just saying "no, it doesn't really matter to me" (if only under our breath) to company domination of our lives. My hope is that once you've detached emotionally, you will start to smile and laugh more, become healthier, and create a positive ripple effect throughout the office environment that will ultimately increase overall corporate innovation and productivity.

Admittedly, it has taken me a while to come around to this way of thinking. I am very pro-business and love to study successful business models—especially the ones that involve innovation and creativity. In a backhanded way that is what brought me to the control-and-fear issue. People who are being controlled are generally neither creative nor innovative, but are more apt to be fatigued and concerned simply about getting through the day. So I believe that once you start the process of detachment, you will not only be happier and more productive, but—and here's the paradox—you are likelier to earn more money from the very company whose psychological control you've managed to escape. For a company to grow requires optimism, innovation, and leadership. The only way you get optimism and innovation is by letting people be themselves in the workplace without undue pressure or stress. That's good leadership.

For a number of years, my advice to people who seemed stressed out by their jobs was to free themselves from company oppression by starting their own business. I have since come around to realizing, however, that many individuals are simply not equipped for such a challenge, or may be too bogged down by economic demands to take a radical step of this nature. My conclusion is that what folks in these situations really need to do is to change their orientation toward their working environment instead—switch to a new 'headset' that's better able to filter out the static and interference that tends to fill the air in corporate surroundings.

That, you might think, is easy for me to say—but this book is intended to make it easy for you to do. It's designed to help you to first become aware of, and then mentally (as well as physically) escape from the psychological traps that corporations instinctively set for jobholders to keep them "in their place"—that is, as few are willing to admit, in a state of passivity, dependency and subliminal fear. Once you've been able to recognize it and emotionally detach from it, I believe you can continue to function within the corporate climate, but in a bolder, more effective, and more meaningful manner. In essence, my approach is one intended to allow you to keep your job while keeping your employer at a distance. By that, I mean no longer able to drain your creative juices, invade your spiritual space, and intrude on your sense of well-being—or, indeed, your sense of self. (Have I got your attention?) My approach will also help you retrieve the personal power that most corporate employees unconsciously relinquish in an attempt to ensure their economic stability by, in effect, sleepwalking through life. When you wake up and retrieve this power, you have the opportunity to change your life. This is something you can do without standing up and telling the world, because most of us are not that bold or outwardly rebellious. You just have to choose to detach emotionally from a callous and calculating culture, and save your emotional attachments for the things that are personally meaningful to you, like your family and your personal mission.

Not only is this the type of plan you can begin implementing right now—it is also one you can utilize to whatever degree best suits you. You need not follow it religiously in order for its benefits to kick in, allowing you to live a happier and healthier life while still inside the corporate structure. And I do mean healthier, in the rehabilitative sense—whether that includes a renewed commitment to improving your physical fitness, reducing the stress-related symptoms and actual maladies that are produced by corporate pressure and intimidation techniques, or a combination of both. What I have also found in working with people is that, in most instances not all of the seven exercises resonate with them, but at least one or two are invariably right on target. The other thing I should mention is that even though some of my recommendations are based on conventional wisdom (e.g., formulating a personal mission and vision), they are presented here in a context all of their own—one that continually emphasizes and reinforces your ability to emotionally detach yourself from a fear-based control environment. (Recently, a V.P. for a major public corporation told me, "I knew I needed a personal mission and to take more time for myself. I just didn't realize how the company I worked for was inadvertently keeping me from doing it. Now I am doing it today.")

Some corporate methodology, such as clarification of a company's mission and vision, can be useful to emulate. Studying this practice can help you formulate a *personal* mission statement. It can also help to sharpen your vision of the greatest person that you ever thought you could be. This personal mission and vision will then offer you a filter by which to prioritize your activities or to-do list on a daily basis, resulting in more free time and less stress. Essentially, these tried and true corporate techniques can be harnessed for the purpose of empowering yourself, which in turn can shield you from fear and control while you go on collecting your paycheck. In other words, they can be instrumental in allowing you to hold on to your job title while also holding on to your personal identity, and not confusing one with the other. Knowing who you really are gives you the ability to stay loose, casual, flexible and spontaneous—in essence, to be yourself, no matter the environment in which you must perform.

Outwardly, the people that comprise the "company" you work for may insist on a formal, rigid code of dress and decorum, and try to keep from making any changes in routine or work flow—even in things as mundane as what time you take lunch, let alone any new creative thought. Strictures of this sort are most apt to be reflected in the "company philosophy"—which, as Marvin Bower observed in an article in *The McKinsey Quarterly*, most commonly "seems to stand for the basic beliefs that people in the business are expected to hold and be guided by—informal, unwritten guidelines on how people should perform and conduct themselves. Once such a philosophy crystallizes, it becomes a powerful force indeed. When one person tells another 'That's not the way we do things,' the advice had better be heeded."[1]

But no matter what the "company philosophy" calls for, it can't keep you from thinking along lines that defy conventional company wisdom (even if you're just imagining yourself coming to the office in shorts, accompanied by your dog). In the exercises that follow, you'll discover a number of different approaches to doing just that—becoming more expansive, open-minded, receptive to the possibilities of a more meaningful existence and able to follow your own higher calling, wherever it may lead.

The first exercise is one designed to give you a sense of direction outside of your job—that is, to help you formulate your personal mission, along with the vision of the person you've always wanted to be. It will provide you with a filter for all your activities, allowing you to prioritize the things that are important to what you've determined to be your mission (or the corporate mission, if the activities are job related).

In the second exercise, you'll discover the importance of separating the time that belongs to your employer from the time that belongs to you and your family—and of using that time to promote your mission, realize your vision, cultivate your talents and get yourself in better physical shape. The recommendations it offers are intended to help you reclaim your life from corporate control, find opportunities to recharge your mental and physical batteries, and cultivate your special skills.

The third and fourth exercises are devoted to ways of psychologically and emotionally detaching yourself from your job and any other controlling situations. These chapters explain how the detachment principle works to make you both a more innovative and productive employee *and* a healthier and happier human being.

Exercise 5 emphasizes the strategic importance of networking and of maintaining a web of contacts—a "collection of connections"—that can help you expand your personal horizons, fulfill your mission, and alleviate your fear of being fired by opening doors to other opportunities.

In the sixth exercise, you'll learn how valuable laughter and a light-hearted attitude are to your physical and emotional health—and how humor can help people in an organization shake off the shackles of fear-based control.

The last exercise is designed to help you share the benefits of your knowledge and experience with coworkers. It will show you the ways in which mentoring can benefit both you and the person you've chosen to mentor, and why it's crucial to have reinforcement—especially from a spouse or partner—in the process of liberating yourself from corporate dominance.

I've been lucky in this respect to be blessed with a wife who's philosophically on my wave length, and thus has been able to contribute to this book by adding her own point of view on each subject. I have also had the advantage of being able to see how well these exercises actually work by talking to many people who have benefited from them (some of whose stories I've incorporated in this book, albeit without revealing their real identities).

Don't get frustrated if you don't see immediate results. Rediscovering yourself and your inner talents and resources and recognizing that you may be working in a controlling, repressing environment is a process that can take months or even years. But, fortunately, you don't have to be stranded alone on an island during that time in order to master the art. It's something you can achieve while you're sitting in business meetings, and engaging in the activities for which you routinely get paid. And the best part is, your corporate bosses will never even realize that you've somehow slipped out of their control because you'll be smiling, laughing and performing at your best, only without the stress. Peers may be startled by the change in your demeanor, and wonder what's up. You'll find that more and more people will gravitate to you, be recommending you for new projects and inviting you to new meetings. In fact, once you've become thoroughly psychologically and emotionally detached, you may even be surprised to find that you get that promotion.

Exercise 1

Be True to Yourself—And Your Mission

*Deciding what you were put on the planet to do
and taking steps in the direction of your dream*

Summary

1. Give yourself a "personal audit" that answers such basic questions as: Why are you on this planet? What are you most passionate about? What are your strengths and weaknesses? Assess how many of your natural inclinations, ambitions, dreams and potentials have been realized. Look at yourself like an entrepreneur in the process of starting a new business venture.

2. Formulate a mission statement that best describes what it is you were put on this planet to do—then focus on accomplishing it.

3. Write down your most incredible vision of yourself—your dream of the way you'd like to be if you could realize your loftiest ambitions. This will become your vision statement.

4. Give yourself a GAP analysis—an assessment of where your life currently is, where you'd like it to be, and five steps you can take to bridge the gap. Then do something every week to advance yourself in that direction.

5. If you work for a controlling company, focus on your true identity, your vision and the mission you've set for yourself. If your job continues to impede your personal progress, set your sights on finding one with an organization whose mission is more compatible with yours

"As long as I can conceive something better than myself, I cannot be easy unless I am striving to bring it into existence or clearing the way for it."
— George Bernard Shaw

"People cannot discover new oceans until they have the courage to lose sight of the shore."
— Anonymous

Imagine yourself being driven in a car with a blindfold on. After a while, you'd find yourself trying to anticipate when the car might make a turn or come to a stop. It would be, to say the least, an uncomfortable feeling of not knowing where you are or where you are going, even though the driver does.

When a person lacks a defined sense of direction, two things are apt to happen. First, someone else fills the void and sends them in a direction not of their own choosing. Second, because they don't really know why they're being steered in this particular direction, they become disoriented and have no idea of where their priorities lay. The result is a stressful, overburdened and unhappy existence.

Every time I found myself being controlled by my boss and driven to complete projects whose purpose I didn't understand or agree with, an uncomfortable feeling came over me, starting deep in the pit of my stomach. The problem was I didn't know where I was going or exactly why I was doing the things on my "to-do" list. Even though I might have had other thoughts or intentions, I surrendered my power to him. I really had no idea of what my purpose was, or even who I was in the scheme of things. Letting the corporation control me led to sleepless nights, bags under my eyes and a general toxicity in my system that was aging me fast. But I continued to do it day after day after day, and couldn't see a way out. In fact, I didn't know I had a problem.

Is that the point at which you, perhaps, now find yourself? Do you know where you're headed, or who you are, or what you're all about? Just asking yourself these questions starts a process of self-realization that keeps pushing you toward finding answers. It's the first step toward achieving a happier and healthier existence that's based on you taking charge of yourself. Such initial self-examination may also be the most difficult step.

If you let other people, such as your boss, or a "company philosophy" determine your destination, you may well end up going around in circles. Comments from colleagues like "that's just the way things are done around here" are merely subtle messages aimed at keeping you from questioning the course that others have plotted for you. Informal, unwritten guidelines on how people should perform and conduct themselves are among the more intimidating methods used to keep you in lockstep. The ultimate purpose of these techniques is to get you to agree to any unrealistic time frame your boss might set to get a project done—or to go along with a policy you know is wrong simply because "he's the boss," even as you leave a meeting saying things like "I can't believe he's willing to sacrifice that amount of share for a price increase." If you think caving in to the system in this manner will make you a happy employee, it's an illusion that should be dispelled right here. Ignoring what you know is right and doing it the company way merely means you have given away your power.

Once you've taken the time to define your mission in life, however, you've already psychologically begun to take them out of the driver's seat, and put yourself firmly at the wheel and in control again. You'll find yourself able to speak up (or at least 'think up') in meetings, having the guts to question unreasonable time frames or bad business decisions. Colleagues will say, "Wow, what's up with him (or her)?" The new respect they'll have for you will empower you further, and interestingly, the fear you had of crossing your boss will dissipate. And once you've done that, and fueled your own personal "think tank" with a vision of the greatest accomplishment of which you might be capable, there are no limits to the places you can go. You'll be energized, grounded and strengthened in your determination to pull off the unique feats you've been put on this planet to accomplish, your existence no longer defined by the things necessary to maintain it, such as "to do" lists, quarterly reports, stock prices or the budget that's due next month. Despite the corporate culture's attempts to convince you otherwise, those things don't represent the real you.

Most people struggle with a personal mission statement. Very successful corporate chiefs have told me that while they have written very successful mission and vision statements for their companies, they never took the time or effort to write one for themselves. Discovering what represents the real you requires looking within yourself, undistracted by the clutter of everyday affairs that so easily commandeers your true sense of purpose. This is not easy in today's world of e-mails, voice mail, faxes and pagers. But it is a crucial step toward personal fulfillment. Just how revealing an experience it can be was demonstrated by an individual who made it the basis of a full-time personal experiment—and whose chronicle of what he found is now regarded as one of history's most profound perspectives on the meaning of existence.

Borrowing a leaf from Thoreau's book

"My purpose in going to Walden Pond," wrote Henry David Thoreau some 150 years ago, " was not to live cheaply not to live dearly, but to transact some private business with the fewest obstacles...to live deliberately, to front only the essential facts of life, and see if I could not learn what it had to teach, and not, when I came to die, discover that I had not lived."

Thoreau was, to put it quite simply, a man on a mission. It was, furthermore, a mission of self-discovery; he sought to understand his place in the natural order of things by stripping away the veneer of material objects and commercial enterprise that respectable society expected of its members, and to live life on its most rudimentary terms.

The mission was one to which he only temporarily devoted himself, residing in his hand-built cabin in the woods for exactly two years, two months and two days. At the time, his purpose in doing so eluded most of his fellow townspeople, and he was during his short lifetime hardly anyone's idea of a successful man—or even a successful author, for that matter. But when it came his time to die, this self-styled Yankee philosopher "died happy." And in the years that followed, his mission ended up having a profound effect on Western ideals.

Needless to say, Thoreau's was not the sort of mission that would suit many of us—he acknowledged as much himself. Even those who might feel similarly inclined would in all probability find such a retreat from civilization and responsibility highly impractical (Thoreau, after all, had no family obligations to concern himself with). But each of us has a mission, whether it be long- or short-term in scope, the nature of which is determined by both our natural inclinations and our particular set of circumstances at any given time. And when we lose sight of our true 'callings' as individuals—most often because we've suppressed our real identities to assume purely artificial ones—an underlying sense of frustration is likely to result, no matter how outwardly successful we may appear.

Where we can all, perhaps, take a leaf from Thoreau's book—even those of us who would no sooner think of taking a woodland sabbatical than flying to the moon—is in the precise and deliberate way he went about formulating his mission statement. True, he may have recorded it for posterity some time after the actual mission was completed—but it's an example that each of us would do well to emulate, no matter what individual course we may follow. Here, after all, was a man who rejected most conventional values—"The greater part of what my neighbors call good I believe in my soul to be bad," he said. Yet he brought to his decidedly unorthodox (some would even say eccentric) mission a sense of clarity, purpose and organization that would have served him well had he opted for the most stereotyped of positions, roles or endeavors. And that, in the end, is what enabled him to transform his personal odyssey into what has since become one of American culture's most highly valued sources of insight and inspiration.

The other lesson we can learn from Thoreau is that a mission is best defined when the mind is cleared of daily clutter. That means going to your own mental "Walden Pond," where you'll be ready to start the process of self-discovery that can bring your personal sense of power back. And from there, you can keep the process moving forward until you too have rediscovered your true self.

A momentous mission born of a chance encounter

Determining one's mission in life needn't always require a deliberate process of self-evaluation. Sometimes, such awareness of what an individual is meant to do may be sparked by some chance encounter or fortuitous experience.

A good example is the case of a 17-year-old English girl from a well-to-do family who was out riding in the country with her clergyman one day when she encountered a local shepherd. Striking up a conversation, she learned that his sheepdog had been injured by some rock-throwing youngsters, and fearing that the dog was permanently disabled, the shepherd thought it best to terminate its life. Determined to assess the situation for herself, the young woman asked her companion to take her to the shepherd's cottage, where they examined the animal and decided its injuries were treatable. Following the clergyman's instructions, she spent the next few days nursing the dog, which responded well to the treatments and was soon back at the shepherd's side. The following night, the young woman dreamt that she heard God's voice directing her on a mission to devote her life to healing others.

Even her family's attempt to divert her in another direction—compiling parliamentary reports—didn't deter her from that purpose, for she took the opportunity to become an expert on the English health-care system. Never allowing herself to lose sight of her mission, seven years later, she began her formal training to carry it out. And that's how Florence Nightingale, "The Lady with the Lamp," came to be known as an angel of mercy to countless sick and wounded soldiers—and the role model for the nursing profession.

A self-audit to answer the question: Why are you on this planet?

"To find yourself, think for yourself."
— *Socrates*

The fact is that no journey can begin, no strategy or planning can be implemented without first knowing where you're going and what outcome you desire. That means developing a mission and a vision that reflects your true self, rather than the way others have attempted to define you. So important is it to find your own sense of direction that the first question I always ask in working either with individuals or with organizations are "For what purpose are you on this planet?"; "What is your mission?" and "What is your passion?" Very rarely can the person, no matter how successful, provide cohesive answers. And although very senior officers of companies can always state the corporate mission, below director level they usually have trouble articulating that mission—and seldom can define one of their own. Yet, an understanding of both your personal mission and the mission of the company you work for is necessary to prioritize your activities. If you know what your mission is, you can do this by asking which of these activities will take you a step closer to accomplishing it. The same holds true for your employer's mission. If you are feeling overwhelmed by job-related activities, ask yourself which ones are most in keeping with the company's mission statement, and use that as a yardstick for prioritizing your to-do list. Taking these simple steps will reduce your stress level. But since this requires that you must first have a clearly defined personal mission, for now, our focus will be on how to go about creating one.

As a first step in your effort to break free from the psychological shackles of the corporation, it's essential that you decide what your real orientation is—what you believe to be your authentic aims in life (or perhaps in its current phase) that reflect the 'true you.'

To do that, I suggest you give yourself a "personal audit"—a written self-assessment of how far you've gone in living up to your natural inclinations, ambitions, dreams and potentials. In other words, try looking at yourself like an entrepreneur in the process of defining a new business venture. Be careful not to prejudge; just 'go with the flow' on this. It may be difficult, at times even painful, but stay with it. Remember: this is a journey of self-discovery that shouldn't be "work"—so if you get bogged down, just move on.

The following are questions to help you in conducting your personal audit:

1. What are you really good at?
2. What are you really passionate about?
3. With whom or what do you most identify?
4. What are your strengths?
5. What are your weaknesses?
6. Do you feel stifled? If so, why?
7. Are there some words, expressions or quotes that you find particularly inspiring?
8. What seeds of greatness or ingenuity might you be harboring, and how far have you gone toward cultivating them?
9. What are your inner resources, and are you—or controlling forces in your life—keeping them from emerging?
10. What words best describe you?
11. Do you live for weekends? If so, why?
12. What identifies and binds everyone around you in a common and worthy pursuit?
13. Do you want to be part of something that can change the world and help make it a better place?

Set these answers aside. We will come back to them in a bit. But first, just one question—when you review the answers, do you already feel lighter and less stressed? If the answer is yes, great!—if not, that's no reason to get frustrated.

Next, go back to when you were eight, nine, ten years old, and try to recall what you thought you were going to be—or the attributes you imagined having—when you grew up. Internalize your thoughts: Did you aspire to become a doctor, an athlete or perhaps an archeologist? Now look at yourself in a mental mirror, and try to honestly evaluate how much you now resemble these ideal—or uncorrupted—visions of yourself. There you have it: the bottom line of your personal audit—the recollection of your childhood ambition or inclinations, along with an evaluation of how you stack up to them in your own mental mirror, not reflected so much in words as in thoughts and emotions. Just write them down as they come. Do not attempt to come to any conclusions or prejudge this yet.

I remember the day I was with one of my favorite long-term clients, who happens to be one of the largest egg distributors in the country. He was becoming fascinated by the way egg yolks could deliver enhanced levels of DHA and Omega 3. As he was laying out the strategy on his white board with four people from his staff present, I noticed a change in his whole demeanor. I could see his face "light up," and his energy level grow and grow. At the end of the meeting, after everyone left, I remarked, "Wow! I have never seen you so jazzed up about anything like this." He replied that it came to him during the meeting that he had always wanted to be a doctor, and when he was discussing the effects of DHA and Omega 3, it felt like he had begun to fulfill his childhood dream.

Now go back to your questionnaire and identify the common theme running through your answers. This information will help you in formulating your mission statement, inasmuch as your mission should be consistent with what makes you tick.

Determining this common theme isn't an easy task, as people tend to shy away from personal definition. In addition, many individuals identify themselves with various artifices—the type of car they drive, for instance (an association consistently supported by television commercials), or what their title is, or how big an office they have. All of which are merely ego-gratifying props, and have nothing whatsoever to do with who we really are or what our actual purpose is in being here. Although there is certainly nothing wrong with having such luxuries or perks, my point is that you should not make the mistake of confusing them with the real you.

So make note of recurring themes—and remember, they are not about your job or title but about the "you" that may be lost underneath it all.

One of the companies I started back in 1995 was a produce systems and procurement operation. One of its major target accounts was a very large quick-service restaurant. The people in the buying office were not very nice, and the buyer's ego had a way of overwhelming everyone who came into contact with him. He would not return calls, and when you did manage to catch up with him, his standard line was, "You have two minutes." A few years later, he had left the company and gone to a much smaller one. This was a difficult adjustment for him. People no longer called him every minute, nor did they bend over backward to see him. When I did talk to him, he had the courage to admit that he had felt like the company's power was his power, and that he was struggling with this. He has since gone back to working for a much larger company. My instinct is that he will now have more than two minutes for people, and my hope for him is that he has succeeded in distinguishing his own power from that of the organization he works for.

Coming to an understanding of who you really are is not something you can accomplish in the time it takes to scan the day's newspaper. It is "pick-and-shovel" work, an ongoing proposition that may not be fully completed for weeks or months (as earlier noted, it took Thoreau more than two years)—and even after that, one that should be the subject of a "refresher course" every so often. But once undertaken, it can be extremely empowering—and liberating. You start to feel better about yourself, to enjoy a sense of greater command over your life, and no matter what seeming difficulties or obstacles you may encounter, you'll view them all from a more focused perspective and a clearer set of lenses. The reason is that you are able to immediately discern the difference between what's important to you and what may be important to someone else. The stress and strain of trying to fulfill someone else's goals can be exhausting and debilitating. Identifying what you are about and what is important to you will empower you.

"You have brains in your head.
You have feet in your shoes.
You can steer yourself any direction you choose.
You're on your own.
And you know what you know.
And you are the guy
Who'll decide where you go."
     — *Dr. Seuss*

Putting your mission into action

Once you complete a self-assessment of who you are and why you're here, you should be better equipped to receive your self-assigned mission. It's a task that calls for you to have all your self-audit notes in front of you—the answers you've given to the questions, the recollections of your youthful aspirations, and your mental-mirror reflections—and to use your instinct for what "feels right" when you've put them all together. Perhaps by now, it's already clear to you what your mission will be—but if it isn't, finding out will require you to administer to yourself yet another "exam." Here's an approach I recommend:

Steps in finding your personal mission

1. In each box below, list a word that describes whatever it is you would be doing right now if money or career were not an issue (for example, "build," "create," "encourage," activate," educate, manage, etc.,) Try to think of at least 25 such words.

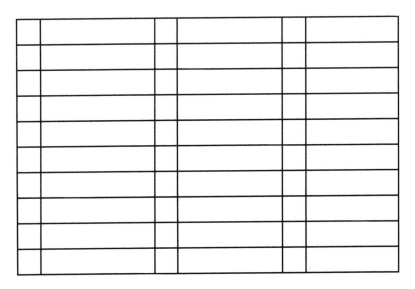

2. Now list the types of endeavors—be they social, cultural, organizational or business-related—that most 'turn you on" (e.g., music, art, motivation, public service, health, environmental protection, etc.). Try to list at least 10.

3. Go back to each list and rate each set on a scale of 1 to 10 with 10 representing the greatest feeling in your heart and soul of what you are about.

4. Put the 10's together in a sentence defining your mission ("My mission is to ____, ____, and ____, in/through ____ and ____.") Try at least five versions.

My mission is to

_____, _____, and] _____,

in/through _____ *and* _____.

My mission is to

_____, _____, and] _____,

in/through _____ *and* _____.

My mission is to

_____, _____, and] _____,

in/through _____ *and* _____.

My mission is to

_____, _____, and] _____,

in/through _____ *and* _____.

My mission is to

_____, _____, and] _____,

in/through _____ *and* _____.

5. Pick three out of the above five. Then narrow it down to one.

_____

_____

_____

Don't hurry—this may take a few days.

I became aware of the importance of a personal mission statement several years ago, when external events beyond my control forced me to redirect my thinking inward. This was some time after I had left a Fortune 500 company and started up several businesses, some of which succeeded and others of which failed (providing some humbling, but useful lessons along the way). Finally, my career as a consultant seemed to have taken off. I had won a lucrative contract doing something that I liked and was good at for a major public company. I had a nice office and a couple assistants in downtown Los Angeles, and had built up an efficient and profitable infrastructure around this consulting arrangement. Life seemed wonderful. True, there had been rumors that all was not well with the corporation involved, but I had dismissed them, because clearly, they had hired me because they needed help. And the underlying health of the industry appeared sound. Then one day, I remember driving up the 710 freeway in Los Angeles and listening to a news report that the company had declared bankruptcy. This wouldn't have been so bad for me, had it not involved the replacement or elimination of the entire management team. That meant my consulting contract was out the window (in fact, I had to fight for back payments owed to me), and within the next four to six weeks, the entire network of interdependent business relationships I had put together slowly began to unravel. The economic rug, so to speak, had been abruptly pulled out from under me. Now what was I going to do? That fear-based feeling was so overwhelming that I can feel it now as if it were gripping me all over again.

As it happened, this was a Fourth of July weekend when my wife had scheduled a trip back to her home town in Illinois, giving me a chance to ponder the question alone with no distractions. So I visited the place where I usually start a lot of my weekends—my neighborhood bookstore—and stocked up on various types of literature I thought might be of assistance. I bought five self-help books offering advice on a range of topics. And I began to realize that while I had conducted many strategic planning sessions for companies, usually on weekends, I had never applied the technique to myself. For the first time, it hit me that I needed my own personal mission and plan—one that a bankruptcy (either my own or someone else's) could not deter me from accomplishing. I realized that I had been a slave to money and all its trappings. My work was judged on the financial outcome it provided. I knew in my heart there had to be more—but it was scary and I wasn't sure I wanted to go there.

In storage I have a strategic planning box, which contains a file of my entire strategic planning seminar, including all the tools and exercises I ask participants in the seminar to complete. I pulled it out, dusted off the files, and thought about my next step. Finally, I mustered enough courage to explore the alternatives, secretly hoping that they wouldn't work. I sat down in the back yard and started to go through the exercises. I started to frame words and phrases on a pad until something resonated with me. The process took a while and involved several different phases, including popping into the box for tools that I had used with senior executives to get them to take a different approach to their business—all the while questioning whether this was the right process for me.

But finally, the beginning of a personal mission emerged—to encourage and inspire myself and others to be more than any of us thought we ever could be. This wasn't something I thought of in terms of a particular industry or type of endeavor, but rather as an overriding objective. Motivating myself or other people was something that 'felt right' for me, and I knew I felt good when I did it. While I wasn't yet sure whether this would be my actual mission, it seemed to meet all the criteria.

A pretty simple mission, really, and probably a little egotistical, but it was the one that honestly seemed to resonate the most with me. So I wrote it down in big letters and taped it to a board that I hung in my home office. Then I proceeded to contemplate how I could carry out this mission—or, more specifically, to evaluate my options in terms of how much they jibed with my newfound sense of what I had been put on the planet to do. Admittedly, the idea of first motivating myself to achieve something greater than I ever thought possible was a bit overwhelming—it would, I thought, be much easier to do for someone else. But the direction was set, and the mission started building momentum as soon as I wrote it down. It was amazing to me how much my energy, which up to then was fragmented, suddenly became focused by this new mission.

As things turned out, before two weeks had passed I managed to line up another anchor client, which interestingly enough had been right in front of my nose but only became apparent to me when my mission stopped being of a purely financial nature. Moreover, the new arrangement was one in which my mission statement played the critical role, rather than the other factors that had been important before, such as the name of the company, the type of project involved and the fee. It seemed that once I had identified a mission for myself, the process of sorting and sifting through various opportunities became a lot easier, and the type of situation I was looking for much clearer. The one I finally set my sights on—and ultimately landed—was with a company whose stewardship had recently passed from father to son. The latter, however, didn't yet know all the ropes, and not wanting to appear ill-prepared to his father, turned to me for help instead. It was the perfect chance to put my mission into action by helping him to successfully build both the business and his self-confidence—an arrangement that continued over the next several years. And in turn, it helped me find the time and energy to motivate myself in areas I had never previously thought were possibilities.

That, however, wasn't the only opportunity I found to fulfill my self-assigned mission. When friends and associates called, I was no longer hesitant to challenge them to scale new heights. I was making a continuous effort to contribute something to everyone I met or spoke to. Then there was my assistant, Susanne, whose own job had been a casualty of my previous reversals. She did, however, have a spark and determination that made her a good subject on which to further culti-vate and test my mission. With some coaching and encouragement, she succeeded in building a business of her own, doing the type of admin-istrative support work for which she was well qualified, and working as an independent contractor for me and others. After just a few years of developing her enterprise, she and three assistants (all at home—either hers or theirs) handle the administrative needs of some 300 hotels. In addition, she continues to run our original food-service sales company and still manages to act as my assistant. She is a person who continues to push herself and grow, in spite of challenges that have included breast cancer (In fact, I could write another book just about her).

Soon, more and more relationships with people began building around "mutual motivations." That is, they would motivate me, and I in turn would do everything I could to motivate them. The ideas and businesses that have since developed from this interaction have encom-passed everything from "healthy" pet food without rendered byproducts to breakfast jerky made from hormone-and-antibiotic-free turkey, and continue to grow in number today. Working with people who have their own sense of mission makes deals and projects easy, quick and rewarding. It also takes the stress out of business relationships because there are no hidden agendas, no facades, no "you only have two minutes."

What guided me most back then was how good the process felt. I took to giving myself regular doses of self-encouragement—egging myself on to follow my natural inclinations, wherever they might lead, discovering what it is I'm destined to do, and doing it better than I ever might have expected I was capable of, setting audacious yearly goals and doing everything I could to accomplish them. Some of these goals I've managed to achieve; others not. In fact, most are now taking longer to bring about because I keep setting the bar higher and higher. At this moment in my life, though, I can tell you I am close to accomplishing one goal I have had for the last 15 years. It has taken five years of work to get to this point, but this would not have happened at all had I not continued to put myself through the self-audit process and refine my personal mission for several years after having first decided to travel down that road.

Like a house, a mission statement is something you're free to remodel whenever the spirit moves you. So a couple years later, I decided that a redesign of mine was in order. Only this time, I came up with a totally different mission—to strive toward the elimination of toxic chemicals in food and the environment. I can't say what it was exactly that prompted me to decide on such a course—perhaps it was a result of all the things I had recently read combined with my personal knowledge of how food is produced and processed. But that was the mission I had set for myself, and that was the direction in which I proceeded. I began by creating a company called Eco-Terra that supported environmentally friendly foods, and went on to steward another enterprise, The New Organics Company, that specialized in organically grown processed foods, including a product line branded with the artist Richard Scary's work appealing to children. And while the latter endeavor didn't prove as economically viable as I might have hoped, it led to two others that have galvanized my enthusiasm. One was initiating and co-authoring a book called *Chemical-Free Kids* (Kensington/Twin Streams Publishing), which for the first time gives parents a comprehensive approach to keeping toxic chemicals out of their children's diet and environment. The other is a project designed to support the viability of family farms and sustainable agriculture, which has brought me close to "The Big Idea"—one that has allowed me to see how amazing it can be when people's personal mission statements align with the organization's, and how a basic structure of principles and values can evolve from that. What is really exciting about this isn't the business angle, but the team concept of like-minded people who now work together. That endeavor—"Family Farm brand"—along with Pet Promise pet food, and this very book, would not have been possible without the fine-tuning of a mission and a group of trusted people to help see it through.

It is important to note that my original mission was never abandoned during this time. Once your mission is embedded in your soul and psyche, the passion you bring to it will exude everywhere. And people from all different places and walks of life will come out to support what you're trying to accomplish.

Imagine where you'd really like to be in life —and start mentally packing!

"If one advances confidently in the direction of his dreams, and endeavors to live a life which he has imagined, he will meet with a success unexpected in common hours."
— *Henry David Thoreau*

"Hold Fast to dreams / for if dreams die / life is a broken-winged bird / that cannot fly."
— *Langston Hughes*

Discovering and refining my personal mission has substantially influenced the course of my journey, and it can similarly empower you. Addressing who you are and what you're here for can lead you to actively embark on the road to self-realization, set your own deadlines and control your own priorities. If you've been keeping up with this exercise so far, you'll have defined your mission. (Can you repeat what it is—right now?) Now the question is—how can you take the necessary steps toward great and meaningful accomplishments? In terms of potential, you're apt to be shortchanging yourself if you focus only on the mission itself. Don't get me wrong: it is the foundation of your newfound sense of personal purpose, and you can stay right there and accomplish more than most people do in their lives, because with purpose and passion, you have power—more power than you might ever have imagined. But I want to throw you one more challenge: *what is the most incredible vision of who you could be?*

Write down the biggest, most far-reaching ambition you could possibly have for yourself. Don't be shy or humble about this. After all, if you were given the opportunity to spread your wings and plan a trip anywhere in the world, would you be content to settle for merely going to a nearby beach or tourist attraction? Or to go coach when you can travel first class? By the same token, you should think of this vision as your chance to take yourself—at least mentally—to the place in life where you would most ideally like to be. Remember, nobody could have become president of the United States without first envisioning themselves in the role. So don't settle for a mediocre picture. The more grandiose or influential, the better.

In shaping your ideal self-image, picture what you'd want to achieve if all things were possible. Imagine realizing your wildest aspiration—for instance, if you're a golfer, becoming a bigger star than Tiger Woods, or if you dabble in art or music, becoming the next Andrew Wyeth or Andrew Lloyd Webber. Or, perhaps, even becoming Time's "Person of the Year."

I, for example, have an "incredible vision" of myself as someone sought out by major corporations such as General Electric and IBM to revamp the structure of their antiquated corporate system, and to dispense advice to their CEOs—like "lighten up, laugh, be more human and give the people working for you room to breathe."

That's the kind of vision you may hear someone refer to as "my fantasy." But (if we may borrow an analogy from the Disney organization), whereas a fantasy belongs in Fantasyland, once you've got the right orientation in the form of self-understanding and a sense of mission, you can transfer yours to the realm of Tomorrowland—and perhaps one day get it to actually take off.

So think of that vision, even if it seems crazy (better yet, in fact, if it is), write it down, absorb it, feel it, smile—you can be that vision. Now we are going to take specific steps to build from the foundation of your mission to accomplish your vision. This is the basic strategic approach used in planning seminars that corporations pay people like me to conduct. But don't get caught in the trap of this becoming just another 'to do' item on the list. This is a life quest, much bigger and more important than any other single task.

Perhaps the most effective way to take stock of yourself and your potentials is to use a process known as GAP analysis. Put simply, it's an assessment of the gap between where and who your are today and who and what you could be in the future—in other words, where you feel your life currently is either personally or professionally, where you'd like it to be, and how you can bridge that gap.

What I recommend is that you write down both your mission and vision on a sheet of paper with the mission in the center and the vision on top. Then below the mission, designate two columns for action steps and the purpose of each step.

Vision:

Mission:

Five steps to move from mission to vision:

	Action		Purpose
1		1	
2		2	
3		3	
4		4	
5		5	

You can begin by writing down five steps that you believe will help get you across that gap—in other words, from where you are today to where you want to be. Put some thought into these. If you were to complete all five, would your vision then become a reality? How about if you just did three? Now the really big question: How do you intend to go about implementing these steps? Your plans for doing so should be quite specific—for instance, looking up Web sites, sending out letters and e-mails, calling or meeting with key people, or acquiring the tools you need to get yourself where you'd ideally like to be. The important thing is to list specific, viable courses of action that can bring about the desired outcomes. And in each case, understand what the purpose of each action step is. Be clear about both the purpose and anticipated results.

Once you've written them down, display them in a place where you'll be sure to see them every day. Then, start doing whatever it will take—even seemingly trivial things—to make each step a reality, and to try to accomplish one or two of them on a daily basis. For example, you can set aside a certain time each day to make phone contacts. Or perhaps your vision involves cultivating some latent skill or talent, as we'll discuss in greater detail in the next exercise on taking time out for yourself—in which case, you might want to "reserve" a special time in the evening to pursue that ambition. If that's not feasible, at least make it your goal to attend to one thing every week—even if it's just one phone call, one e-mail or perhaps brainstorming with your spouse or partner. The important thing is to stay with it. You might be amazed at the doors such perseverance can potentially open. Pay attention to all the things that can reinforce your vision and help you get your mission under way. Now you may be asking yourself "how will I ever get to those to-dos?" This is the remarkable blessing of this exercise. Whenever you feel stressed out from work, or your job is overwhelming you, stop, take a break, and work on one of the above steps. You may be surprised at how effective this can be at alleviating stress, lightening your load and recharging your energy. For example, looking up a Web site for more information you can use to bring you closer to your vision—this small act can help liberate you from the command and control of the typical corporation and restore your personal power. Just make sure everything you do is somehow consistent with your mission—including (if necessary) taking steps to position yourself with a company whose mission is more in keeping with your own.

"There is no passion to be found playing small—in settling for a life that is less than the one you care capable of living."
— *Nelson Mandela*

Is there a job out there that jibes with your mission?

The job you're doing need not be at odds with your inclinations— or something you'd necessarily want to quit if you actually did get your hands on that lucky lottery ticket. Once again, it's all a question of how well what you're doing jibes with your personal mission—and if it doesn't, how successful you can be at finding something that's more in keeping with that mission (which even a lottery winner needs to define, especially once having been relieved of the daily burden of making a living).

One of the key things your initial self-assessment should reveal is the relationship of your work to your feeling of validity and your true aim in life. Just as some people can live practically anywhere while others only feel comfortable in a particular type of locale or climate, there are those who seem able to adapt to any type of employment environment and others who may feel terribly constrained and unhappy in the wrong type of job. If you are one of the latter, it wouldn't at all surprise me to learn that the prospect of long-term employment in a large publicly owned corporation doesn't exactly thrill you.

Having had considerable experience working in both a corporate environment and with small, independent start-up companies, I find the contrast in employee morale nothing short of amazing. For more often than not, what characterizes the large corporate structure is a failure on the part of thousands of employees to understand either its mission or any principals or core values arising from it. But such a lack of understanding is understandable when one realizes that there is apt to be no corporate mission other than generating as much profit for stockholders as possible. It could very well be that no matter what such a company is producing or selling, it's actually driven by nothing but earnings per share. Recently, a vice president for a medium-sized private company told me in the course of an interview that he did not trust the CEO to look out for his or anyone else's job. He asserted that if someone from the company were to be hit by a car, the CEO's only response would be, "I hope it wasn't in the company parking lot."

Interestingly enough, that's not apt to be what the entrepreneurs who started these companies had in mind. One such founder, in fact, told me that he could never have built the company he did had its present profit motive been the only objective. He seemed to take pride in the fact that the firm had not even turned a profit during the first seven years of its existence. When I spoke with him, it was in its 11th year as a public company, only in his mind, the values and principles it had been founded on had not changed. The biggest concern he voiced to me was that the profit motive and stock options were wringing the soul out of his company right before his eyes.

The smaller, privately owned companies I have worked with, on the other hand, were the ones that managed to communicate a sense of mission, principals and values to their employees. And I could always sense that the people who worked for those companies took far more pride in their jobs, were more willing to volunteer, and were generally more enthusiastic about their role.

No job, of course, should dominate an individual's existence to the point where life would lose its meaning should it suddenly disappear. The attitude that "the company is my life" is an unhealthy one that should be avoided under any circumstances (as I hope this book will make clear). But the right working environment can help to validate one's sense of personal identity and mission. When this happens, it is magic. I recently had dinner with an individual who had struggled with different jobs for 15 years before going to work for a company that is nurturing, honest and provides great opportunities for growth. Spending time with him was energizing and restored some of my confidence in what the corporate sector is capable of when enlightened people are in charge. Companies that recognize the value of their "off balance-sheet" assets—their employees—are the ones with which you will have your best chance of linking your personal mission.

Benefits and profit-sharing programs, such as the precedent-setting one offered by Starbucks, are key indicators as well. Its effectiveness becomes apparent when Starbucks founder Howard Schultz comes into a meeting and relates story after story of the extraordinary things that have been accomplished by store employees.

By contrast, one of the largest grocery retailers in the country didn't even mention its employees as one of its top five assets in the company's 2002 annual report. (I received no response from the CEO when I wrote him and asked him why). One has to wonder about the values system of a service-based retailer that holds the people who work for it in such low esteem.

Apart from everything else, valuing employees is just plain good business. As Steve Horowitz, a friend and highly respected consultant, tells other businessmen, it's people that represent a company's most important asset—even if they can't be listed as such. "If there's one quality that separates the winning companies from the losers," he observed, "it's their people and the ability of management to bring out the best in them." That's because "90 percent of the knowledge in any company lies with the people doing the jobs. They see what's working and what's not." But there's usually no incentive for them to try to facilitate change, he notes, "since most corporations believe that all decisions have to be made 'at the top.'

Not that everyone who's discontented in a job can necessarily make the switch to a more ideal situation that easily. Nor can most of us simply retreat to the woods, like Thoreau. That's why it's so important to formulate your own sense of mission and to develop strategies to sustain it while continuing to function in that corporate command-and-control atmosphere.

The point is for you to "become your own person" with both a mission and a vision that are impervious to institutional or corporate control—whether or not they're consistent with the aims of the organization you serve. If you can succeed in doing that, congratulations—you're on your way to a happier, healthier and more fulfilling life.

Your next mission: clearing some space for the one you've decided on

If you've successfully completed Exercise One, you'll have given yourself a personal audit, assessing your inclinations, dreams, potentials, strengths and weaknesses, and used it to formulate a mission statement that best describes what it is you were put on this planet to do. You'll also have defined your most ideal vision of yourself—your dream of the way you'd like to be if you could realize your loftiest ambitions—and embarked on five steps you can take to bridge the gap between where you are now and where you'd ideally like to be in life.

Assuming you've accomplished all that, you're already way ahead of the game in terms of living a life that's truly satisfying despite continuing to work within a corporate culture whose climate is apt to remain fear-based and controlling.

The trick is to keep that corporate environment from undermining your newfound resolve, your enthusiasm for your mission and your health. In the ensuing exercises, you'll learn some more techniques for taking back your personal power—starting with keeping your bosses from encroaching on the "personal time" you'll need to devote to your mission, your vision, your family and your well-being.

"Things that matter most should never be at the mercy of things that matter least."
— *Goethe*

Reflections: Exercise 1

Was the personal audit easy or difficult for you? Is this a new process for you, or something you've been working on for a while?

_____

_____

_____

_____

_____

_____

_____

Does your mission statement surprise you at all? Why or why not?

_____

_____

_____

_____

_____

_____

What is the most significant step you will take in order to fulfill your personal mission? At work? At home?

_____

_____

_____

_____

Do you anticipate working toward your personal mission to be an easy or difficult process? Do you foresee any major obstacles? If so, what is the main one?

_____

_____

_____

_____

Exercise 2

Reclaim the Time that Belongs to You

Finding room for the things that will strengthen your inner resources

Summary

1. Start with a new attitude—that your personal needs and requirements are every bit as important as those of your employer, and that you owe as much to yourself, your family and your personal mission as you do to your job.

2. Prioritize your to-do lists of both job-related and mission-related tasks.

3. Put yourself on a fitness program of daily exercise—above all, regular walking, which can help prevent heart disease, cancer and diabetes, boost your overall health, help control your weight, ward off depression and sharpen your mental capabilities.

4. Do other things to improve your physical state, like switching to a healthier diet, cutting out fast food and diet soda, taking supplements, and seeing a chiropractor who specializes in wellness.

5. Give your creative abilities a jump start by actively engaging in whatever it is you have any special talent at—be it playing a musical instrument, writing, painting, crafting furniture, or whatever.

6. Do things to further your education in areas of interest or related to your mission, whether they involve taking courses and studying for an advanced degree, or such informal approaches as reading, attending lectures, plays and concerts, or listening to tapes and CDs that can enhance your knowledge.

"Make the most of yourself, for that is all there is of you."
— *Ralph Waldo Emerson*

Have you ever run into a former colleague who either quit or was laid off from his or her job, and noticed that the person looked considerably better—perhaps younger and more relaxed—than he or she did at the office? Sure, this individual might be facing a whole new set of problems, like the daunting task of finding another job. But in the meantime, it's a good bet that this person is also going regularly to the gym, finding time for their family, rekindling interests or skills long put on hold, and in their own way, rediscovering who they really are.

A real-life situation provided me with much of the original inspiration for this book. A former colleague of mine—I'll call him Clark—had gone through a tough year with a boss who was trying to mold him into what *he* wanted as opposed to Clark's running a marketing program the way Clark knew how. This led to many confrontations, and Clark was becoming tired and worn. He was working too many hours and on too many things he didn't feel were important. When it all finally came to a head and Clark resigned, I was deeply disappointed, having known Clark to be extremely talented and feeling that the team had lost a valuable player.

A couple weeks after his resignation, we arranged to meet for coffee. When Clark walked up, I didn't recognize him. "Wow," I said, "you look 10 years younger." "That's what everyone has been saying," he replied. The realization of just how negative an impact a controlling CEO could have on a competent employee had a profound effect on me. I suspected there were a good many Clarks out there in the corporate world, and what they needed was a set of principles for keeping its counterproductive influence from undermining their quality of life. I began to formulate the exercises in this book the very next day.

The corporate command-and-control culture has the unique ability to run you ragged and potentially physically eat away at you from the inside out, if you let it. The only way you can keep it from doing so, other than quitting your job, is to take your power back by building your own defensive barrier against fear and control. Indeed, you have already taken a giant step toward that objective if you have succeeded in identifying who you really are and determining your life's mission and vision. This should already have endowed you with a new attitude that you do have a life apart from the demands of your employer, and a right to aspire to the greatest thing you ever dreamed you could be, rather than just a corporate cog.

You don't need to give your boss—or any one, for that matter—a formal declaration of your intention to do so. But you will need the strength and resolve to stay 'on mission' and not be deterred from your purpose. That means you'll need to get moving and put yourself on a physical fitness program—one that includes regular walking, healthier eating, vitamin and mineral supplements—and start shaking off those unhealthy living habits (something that should be easier once you've cut down on job stress). Nothing could be more important to the success of your mission and to becoming more productive and healthier than getting yourself physically rehabilitated. You will need stamina to meet all your new personal goals. But that doesn't mean that just because you used to run three miles a day, you can automatically pick up where you left off—as many heart-attack victims have discovered too late. Working your way back to health should be a gradual process, beginning with and switching to healthier foods and taking regular walks. Just the act of getting moving will imbue you with a positive new feeling.

Are there other activities that you have set aside because of a lack of time or energy, such as a musical instrument you've been keeping in the closet for 20 years? If so, your next step might be to dust it off and start playing again. Or maybe you can get going with some creative outlets you've often dreamed of pursuing. Or how about catching a lecture, or simply reading a book—anything you wouldn't have had time to do while your efforts, focus and commitment were totally commandeered by your employer (or anyone else). When you're feeling good, it's much harder for anyone in the corporate command-and-control structure to 'drive your bus' or assert its dominance over you. At the same time, you're bound to be more proficient at doing your job, as well as more innovative, creative and just plain fun to be around.

The only way you can be true to your mission—and, hopefully, realize your vision—is by allowing yourself the time, the energy and the feeling of well-being to see it through. That might sound tough to do when so much of your time, effort and dedication is going into meeting someone else's demands or those of your corporate job. But once again, a helpful thought on the subject can be found in the writings of one of the sages of America's history—the same guy, as it turns out, who could combine a historic mission of discovery with flying a kite.

All work and no play makes for an unhealthy waste of time

"Dost thou love life? Then do not squander time, for that's the stuff life is made of." At first glance, that bit of advice from Benjamin Franklin might sound like a recommendation that we keep our noses to the grindstone. But that would hardly seem to be what a free spirit like Franklin would advocate—nor the way anyone should interpret that statement who's the least bit creative, innovative, happy to be alive (as Franklin was) and not psychologically bound by a Puritan work ethic (Franklin as a young man having chosen to flee the staid, puritanical atmosphere of Boston for more flamboyant locales).

Sure, work is a necessary component of survival (assuming you're not the heir to some large fortune or lucky enough to hold the winning six numbers in a state lottery). But there's a point beyond which labor becomes counterproductive when it squanders the time one should be devoting to other essential activities. People who give too much of their time to their jobs are allowing their lives to be largely wasted. An unrelenting work schedule can be as destructive to well-being as any other form of overindulgence (hence the term "workaholic"), and being constantly overworked can literally be as unhealthy as being overweight (with both conditions, in fact, often being directly related).

A recent study published in *Psychosomatic Medicine* found that being powerless at work tends to increase a person's blood pressure, an added risk factor for heart attacks and strokes. This jibes with research done by the American Institute of Stress (to be discussed in Exercise 3) showing a correlation between symptoms of stress and the feeling of powerlessness.

When you have a job, you're expected to give a certain amount of your time (as well as effort and expertise) to your employer in exchange for a paycheck and benefits. While the standard full-time job is supposed to involve eight-hour days and 40-hour weeks (reduced by half-an-hour per day in many firms to allow time for lunch), the increased emphasis on bottom-line performance displayed by many corporations has rendered that standard largely meaningless. Instead of the benefits of technology having given us a shorter work week, as some pundits had predicted they would, many of us, ironically, are now faced with the opposite situation—seemingly compelled to sacrifice more and more of our time to the companies that employ us.

The luckier among us can at least expect to be additionally compensated for such exploitation in the form of overtime pay. Others may find themselves in the less fortunate position of having to "eat those hours," thanks to job descriptions that limit pay—but not the amount of time required by the job—to 40 hours a week. One vice president of marketing for a major automobile company told me that it was unrealistic for him not to work 12-hour days and a good part of the weekend. His explanation was, "If I don't, somebody else will, and I'll be replaced."

In either case, however, you end up robbing yourself by reducing the quality—and perhaps even the length—of your life when you devote all, or most, of your waking hours to satisfying the demands of a profit-driven corporation. What's more, when you starve the rest of your existence in this manner, your work performance is bound to suffer. The quality of your thinking, your energy and stamina, will be zapped. As advertising magnate David Ogilvy put it, "If your creatives are in the office, you have a problem." Nor is "retirement" apt to alleviate the effect, as indicated by the substantial number of people who die within a relatively short time of retiring. When a person devotes all their time and energy to a job and it's suddenly gone, they may feel like an empty vessel with nothing left to live for. Worn out from years of unremitting toil and without having nurtured hobbies, passions and other skills or interests outside of the workplace, they may find little of interest to sustain them and eventually just "give up."

Becoming a workaholic, which is the norm today, has the effect of diminishing you as a person. When you become a virtual slave to your job or to someone else, it's easy to lose sight of your true identity, your natural talents and inclinations, and whatever mission you might have been intended for on the planet.

"I realized one day that I'd given my career control over my life, and now I wanted the control back"
— *Deborah Norville*

If that's the position you find yourself in, what you need to do is not so much to "get a life," as the popular expression goes, but to get your life back. And that means reclaiming the time that's being stolen from you by your corporate overseers and using it to serve other needs that are every bit as compelling and important as your work. This is where prioritizing in accord with your mission can be especially helpful. What I would suggest is that you re-evaluate your to-do list. Are the job-related items consistent with the company's mission? Will the personal ones serve to further your own mission and vision? When you do this, you'll find yourself breathing a sigh of relief, because you'll have narrowed your focus to only what's important and meaningful— and stop devoting so much time to superfluous activities that benefit neither you nor the company you work for.

One of my clients, a small public company, had spent a couple years cutting every cost and invoking every efficiency measure it possibly could to maintain its earnings per share. The management team was overworked and micro-managed at every level. No one looked healthy or vibrant—just beat up. I was in their office about a month after the firm had been acquired at a terrific premium. I asked one of the VPs how it was going, and he replied, "It's going great. The company is running better than ever because without the pressure of quarterly earnings, we are all able to focus on the important stuff and not chase all the minutiae." That pretty much said it all.

Giving 'equal time' to your own requirements

When I urge you to take time out for yourself, I'm not talking about the hours you spend at your child's soccer game or having dinner with your parents. The importance of devoting time to your family can't be emphasized enough, but it's in a category all of its own (although sometimes, it's possible to combine family and personal time in mutually beneficial ways). I'm also not referring to things like the way an otherwise diligent former business associate of mine used to occasionally blow off steam by gambling nonstop for 48 hours in Las Vegas. Certainly, frivolous activities such as partying have their place (although not necessarily gambling junkets, unless you can afford to lose), but they're not the purpose of the specific periods of time I recommend allowing yourself each week. Those should be for improving your body, mind and spirit—in essence, for strengthening your inner resources. Nothing is more critical than setting aside this personal time to rejuvenate and recharge your batteries.

But how, exactly, do you go about doing that? It starts with your attitude—the conviction that you did not agree to sell your soul to anyone else for a salary, and that you owe yourself "equal time" for your own requirements and your personal mission, which are more important than your employer's to-do list (not only to you, but perhaps to others that your mission may benefit, which may ultimately include your employer). Once you've latched onto this realization, you'll somehow start making room in your schedule for the things you have to do to align with your mission, as well as to increase the quality—and in all likelihood the length—of your life. The paradox is that making more time for yourself and your mission can't help but make you a better employee, as well as spouse, parent—and person.

In a sense, you have to think of yourself as if you were your own union representative—renegotiating the terms not only of your employment, but your life. You have to set limits on what's expected of you in your job, and by the same token, expect more of yourself in other areas, including the mission you've set for yourself. This is not an anti-corporate tactic, but a strategy for achieving a happier and healthier life in which everyone wins—you, your family, and your employer (by having a more productive and creative employee).

Time yourself

Approximately what percentage of your time do you give each day to the following? What would you like it to be?

1. Mission _____ _____
2. Hobbies _____ _____
3. Family/Friends _____ _____
4. Reading/Education _____ _____
5. Physical exercise _____ _____
6. Employer/Work _____ _____
7. Sleep _____ _____

What is the percentage of hours in a typical weekday that are consumed by work and sleep? What percentage would you like it to be? What are you going to do to change it? Remember, by focusing on your mission, you will be able to determine what's important and start using that as the barometer of how this time should be spent. Put this chart next to your mission and vision chart where you can see it often. If more than 40% of your time is devoted to work, you should start making adjustments immediately. If work and sleep combined come to 80%, you have no life.

I believe that in a perfect world, an average weekday would include eight hours of work and eight hours of sleep. The remaining third of the day—along with the entire weekend—should be yours, giving you sufficient time for exercise, hobbies, reading, your family and your mission. No one ever thought that people could commute for an hour or more each way and be simultaneously engaged in company business. What about your commute? Are you on the cell phone conducting business while going to and from work? Is that time yours or your employer's? Can't today's companies survive with their employees working eight-hour days? A CEO of a billion-dollar company that I did a project for left every day at 5 p.m., no matter what. Guess what? Everyone knew it, and respected and accommodated that schedule. I know you're thinking, "So what—that's the CEO." Well, if you perform efficiently, you can accomplish the same thing. Remember, it's the performance that counts. Focusing on what's important, rather than a to-do list for the sake of a to-do list, can enable you to accomplish an awful lot in eight hours.

Here's a suggestion. Instead of just a conventional to-do list, write your list based on the result you would like to achieve. For example, "Take car in for an oil change" would become "Make sure I have a way to get around in the future." Or "call account" might instead be "Develop relationship with the buyer." Or "Look up Web site on photography " might translate into "Learn all you can about photography's core principles." Then prioritize these desired outcomes as they relate to either your personal or corporate mission. For example, if field sales and account calls are what you need to accomplish to fulfill your company's mission, then getting your car serviced is high on the priority list. If taking good pictures is crucial to your personal mission, that might also head the list, whereas things like mowing the lawn and washing the car might be given a much lower priority (unless, of course, the appearance of the car was important to your image when you made sales calls). Once you've prioritized both your work-related and personal tasks in this manner, you might be amazed at how much more you can get done in the course of a regular work day.

Focusing on those activities related to your personal mission and the company's mission first will free up a tremendous amount of time and alleviate that sense of being overwhelmed, making you both feel better and perform better.

Walking your way back to health—and happiness

Recently, a very good friend of mine suffered a mild heart attack, which he regarded as a wake-up call. He subsequently began an exercise program, lost a significant amount of weight, and began to look and feel 10 years younger. And interestingly enough, devoting more time to his own well-being didn't interfere with his productivity.

You don't have to reach a crisis point, such as my friend did, to realize that by spending your life in a sedentary, stressful job, you're making yourself a target for killer diseases. You owe yourself—and your family—the benefits of being in good condition. But staying healthy is something you've literally got to exercise your right to do. No matter what other changes you initiate to improve the shape you're in—eating healthier foods, cutting down on the size of your portions—you've simply got to "get moving." It doesn't really matter how—just move it!

The great thing about exercising, however, is it doesn't necessarily require working out, joining a gym or taking up a sport like tennis or racquetball. All it takes is your two feet. If there's one thing that today's health researchers all agree on, it's that nothing beats walking for keeping yourself physically fit. "I'm convinced from the research that a sedentary lifestyle kills you, and moderate activity like walking can be a lifesaver," says JoAnn Manson, a professor of medicine at Harvard Medical School and chief of Preventive Medicine at Brigham and Women's Hospital in

Boston. Manson recommends 'walking your way' up to at least 10,000 steps a day—something you can measure by wearing a pedometer, or step counter, on your waistband.[2]

And what's most advantageous about walking is that you can go at your own pace. You neither have to run (a strenuous activity that is not recommended for a lot of people), "power walk," or "take a hike" in order for positive effects to kick in. Studies have shown that the benefits of moderate walking—that is, going a couple miles in 30 or 40 minutes—are practically identical to those one gets from "race walking" at 10 or 11 miles a minute. In addition, you can break up your walks—taking them in, say, four 15-minute segments per day—and achieve the same results as walking for a straight hour.

Here are some of the reasons why it takes all the walking you can do to stay in shape:

1. Regular walking has been shown to improve cardiovascular health by, among other things, helping to maintain the elasticity of blood vessels, improving the heart's pumping capacity, stabilizing blood-pressure levels, reducing your resting heart rate and increasing HDL (good) cholesterol.

2. Walking is a good way to alleviate depression, anxiety and stress. In other words, it really does help to 'walk off' the blues or the pressures of your job.

3. Walking can genuinely help you to become more productive and creative—both in your work and in other aspects of life—by increasing blood flow to the brain. In fact, a study funded by the National Council on Aging found that people over 60 exhibited better ability to think and higher degrees of mental sharpness after working themselves up to walking 45 minutes a day at a pace of 16 minutes per mile.

In addition to the benefits of longer life, better health, a happier outlook and a clearer mind, walking has the advantage of being either a solitary or a social activity. It's something that you can do with a spouse, significant other or your kids—one of those opportunities to devote time to both self-improvement and family togetherness.

Thanks to today's communication technology, you can also conduct business while out for a stroll. For instance, I make it a point not only to walk at least 45 minutes every day, no matter where I am or what I'm doing, but quite often to talk while I walk via cell phone. In fact, it's my preferred way to engage in conference calls.

In addition, walking gives me a chance to get to know—or become reacquainted with—the various locales that I visit. Previously, when I would travel to St. Louis, I would make it a habit to schedule as many meetings there as I could, taking it to the extent of going through my Rolodex and seeing who I might arrange to meet with as long as I was there—sometimes squeezing in four or five such meetings in a day. The result was that after two or three days of this self-imposed grind, I would wind up feeling extremely fatigued. Now, I won't say I don't still revert back to doing this on occasion—old habits, after all, are hard to break—but now, I make sure I leave at least 45 minutes open to walk the downtown. And if this is inconvenient, I at least try to spend 45 minutes or an hour in the hotel gym, mostly on the treadmill.

Of course, I engage in other forms of physical activity as well—especially regular workouts in the form of kick boxing three or four times a week. But those walks are the mainstay of my personal "health maintenance plan." It's amazing how much these interludes of physical activity enable me to handle the complexities of the day!

In addition to walking your way back to health, there are other things you can start doing to take better care of yourself and improve your physical condition. I would recommend, for instance, that you consult a holistic chiropractor, or one who practices wellness, get some neurological testing done, and determine what treatments or supplements you might need to boost your immunity and alleviate certain problems or deficiencies that might be hindering your well-being. You should also take a close look at your dietary habits, realizing that there is a lot of truth in that old saying "You are what you eat." By that standard, you'll be at your best by eating whole foods, meaning foods that are not processed—or processed foods such as bread that are made from whole grains. Whenever possible, you should try buying organic foods and taking regular supplements of vitamins and minerals and a green drink of spirulina (a beneficial algae) along with DHA and Omega 3—making sure they are from whole-food sources, not synthetic ones. Eliminating fast foods, diet soda (which contains aspartame, an ingredient that can cause such side effects as headaches and vision problems) and toxic chemicals from your diet can make a major difference in your overall health. A regimen of regular walking combined with unadulterated whole foods can make an amazing difference in your outlook and ability to think and perform, as well as increase your overall energy level. Above all, this will give you the physical strength to take your life back from a controlling situation or a controlling company.

But to do all that, you've got to stay focused on what's important.

In a controlling environment, it takes strength not to allow petty concerns to divert you from the business of making yourself stronger and healthier. You've got to exercise your right to exercise—and to eat the kinds of food that will help restore your physical and mental power.

Stress-busters to the rescue

In a study of British men 18 to 42 years old, University of Birmingham researchers found that those taking daily doses of a multivitamin supplement high in vitamin C and all the B vitamins registered a 21 percent drop in anxiety levels, felt less tired and were more focused, while stress actually seemed to increase among those taking a placebo (no word on what that placebo contained). The results were in keeping with other research showing that such vitamins help to reduce stress.

Toxic food and toxic people: an unhealthy combination

Toxins in food have a lot in common with fear and control. The former create wear and tear on your cells, and can age you as your body expends its energy to store up the impurities they contains. The latter can have a similar effect on your physical well-being, whether you opt to roll with or confront them. But you can choose not to eat toxic food, and you can detach yourself emotionally from toxic people to the point where they no longer get inside you (a process we'll discuss in the next exercise).

There's no time like the present to find out how gifted you are

Once you have restored your energy with a healthier diet and regular exercise, the next step in taking back your life from corporate control is to make use of your special talents. The desire to create something unique, meaningful or beautiful, and thus to leave a lasting impression of one's existence, is practically universal. But most people's employment provides little opportunity to do anything that reflects their creativity or individuality. This is especially true when one is a cog—even an important cog—in a large-scale corporate culture. That's one reason why devoting too much time to a job, leaving little room for other activities, is apt to result in feelings of deep-seated frustration.

The corporation man (or woman) who takes time to nurture some natural creative ability, on the other hand, is apt to find the job far less oppressive and stressful.

You probably know in which direction your creativity flows, whether you have some particular artistic abilities or inclinations, or some special type of inventiveness or ingenuity. You may have to think back to high school or college to activities or artistic endeavors you've since allowed to become dormant. Or maybe you've attempted to develop them, only to be too distracted by responsibility and job demands to give them much of your attention. Whatever the case, and no matter how successful you may be in your chosen profession, you're likely to go on feeling unfulfilled and dissatisfied unless you put those God-given talents to use. I am always amazed to go to a colleague's home and discover that he or she has some extraordinary talent or distinction that nobody in the office has a clue about. Who could have guessed that someone with whom you worked every day had once been a child movie star, or was a champion gymnast, or a disc jockey? Those are the types of things I have discovered about co-workers at various times—and are what stands out in my mind whenever I think of them, rather than the positions they occupied in the company.

Have an impulse to draw or paint? Find the time to do so—and get busy putting together a portfolio of your work, or matting or framing it for display in your home (and who knows—maybe someday, a gallery). Have a natural flare for writing? Don't just waste it on corporate reports that will ultimately end up gathering dust or being shredded—get to work on some articles, short stories, poetry, or perhaps a novel. Then submit your efforts to magazines, newspapers or publishing houses (and don't be discouraged by rejection slips, which are all but inevitable unless you're famous). An ear for music—and perhaps some knowledge of a particular instrument like the guitar, piano or saxophone? Then start practicing—even if it means having to learn it from scratch. (A client of mine in the produce business is often known to play his guitar for the benefit of the entire office at the end of a stressful work day. It makes the employees smile and gives the place a real "happy family" feeling.) A knack for building and crafting things? Get those tools out and start designing some pieces for the house (maybe you'll even start a business on the side). Or perhaps you have the proverbial green thumb. Get out in the fresh air and brighten up the neighborhood with your flower beds—or give your family the benefit of cheaper, better quality food by starting your own organic vegetable garden.

Whatever you accomplish, it's something that will be representative of your unique, personal identity—a way of proving to yourself and the world your true validity and value unaffected by the fickleness and fortunes of corporate culture.

Such self-enrichment, involving your native abilities and inclinations, may well be part of your mission in life—or provide you with a means of carrying it out. A perfect illustration is cartoonist Scott Adams, whose own experiences with corporate craziness fueled his talent for conceiving satire—with the result being the wildly popular comic strip, "Dilbert" (you'll find more about him in Exercise 6 : Lighten Up).

Sometimes you have to pull back in order to get ahead

When I was affiliated with a relatively large private company, I used to notice that at least a couple times a week, the CEO, who was a friend of mine, would take an unusually long lunch break. He'd leave around 12:30 and not get back until almost 3 or 3:30. But it wasn't until years later that I found out where he disappeared to during that time. It wasn't to a restaurant, but to a local movie house. The cinema, it seems, was a special hobby of his—he loved movies, knew everything about the industry, and could critique actors as far back as you could imagine. So catching the latest flick in the middle of the day went beyond just going to the movies—it was his way of keeping on top of the industry's latest offerings, and thus continuing to educate himself in a field that really "turned him on." And I think taking time off in the middle of the day to do that improved his outlook, and put him in far better fettle to handle his business responsibilities.

Just as engaging in creative endeavors is an active way of enhancing your value to yourself and others—and often carrying out your mission in the process—furthering your education can be a passive method of achieving the same result. It's also something you can do on either a formal or informal basis. You can opt to take courses and perhaps even work toward an advanced degree, or you can indulge in your own informal type of learning experience, as did my movie-going friend.

There are a number of ways you can go about acquiring new information and insights without having to attend classes. Reading, of course, is top on the list (and something that you are obviously into already), particularly now with so much information available on virtually every topic via books, articles and the Internet. There are also lectures you can attend on a wide range of subjects, as well as plays, concerts, museums and galleries. Some of the more informative and entertaining opportunities along these lines, in fact, can be experienced at some of today's mega-bookstores, which often feature appearances by contemporary writers and some excellent up-and-coming musical talents. that patrons can attend free of charge (and which you can enjoy with your entire family as part of the time you share with them).

Tapes and compact discs can also be used for myriad self-education purposes, from learning foreign languages to hearing excerpts from recent books—often in the author's own voice. Or they can always be used for the more traditional purpose of acquainting yourself with new or unfamiliar musical compositions—particularly the classics, which bear repeated hearing in order to fully appreciate (listening to classical music being an excellent form of both stress relief and mental stimulation). The beauty of audio technology, of course, is that it provides a form of both learning and enjoyment you can indulge in while commuting to and from work—making optimal use of those hours when you're stuck in traffic, and hence allowing you to follow Franklin's dictum about not squandering time.

Driving, in fact, can be one of the best ways of taking time for yourself. When I travel these days, I make it a point to put some "arrival distance" between myself and my ultimate destination. For instance, whenever visiting a client of mine in Boulder, Colorado, I deliberately stay in Denver so as to give myself the advantage of a 40-minute ride to just unwind and collect my thoughts.

Lastly, one of the best ways I recommend to make time for yourself is to be an early riser. If you're in the habit of waking up at 7, try getting up at 6 and finding someplace—perhaps your kitchen, or a coffee shop—where you can prepare for the day in an unhurried way. I use that private morning time, for instance, to write in my journal at least three or four times a week. What I've discovered is that an unhurried start to the day, free of distractions and static, is an ideal time for introspection. This is also the time I review my to-do list as it relates to my mission. It is simply amazing how much better one's days seem to go when they include such time set aside for quiet contemplation.

So far, so good—now are you ready to neutralize the control module?

Let's see just how far you've come. You've got a mission in life, along with a vision of the greatest thing you might be capable of accomplishing. And you've begun to take back your life in a variety of ways—by getting yourself in better shape, physically and mentally, developing the gifts and talents you might have been neglecting, discovering how creative you are, and continuing your education, either formally or informally.

But you've still got a job with someone attempting to control you in a corporate environment, and you're in no position to walk away from that. So next, you're ready to discover the power of detachment—that is, the way that emotionally detaching from one's job and employer, along with a sense of personal mission, can actually restore one's ability to be innovative and productive at work as well as to be a healthier and happier person.

When you're off on a trip, best to stay off line

I've quit traveling with a laptop, having come to the conclusion that e-mail is one of the biggest inhibitors of your ability to make time for yourself. Feeling obliged to answer a bunch of messages (perhaps 50 or 60 per day, in my case), and concerned that if I didn't there would be twice as many the next day, was simply eating up whatever time I might have allowed myself to regroup after a day of meetings or seminars. My advice to fellow travelers: if at all possible, leave the computer at the office.

All work, no sleep puts you at risk of a heart attack

Men working more than 60 hours a week had double the risk of having a heart attack of those who worked 40 hours or less in a recent study by Japanese researchers.

The study, whose results were published in the journal *Occupational and Environmental Medicine*, involved hundreds of Japanese men, including some who had suffered heart attacks and others who had not. The results were adjusted so that other risks, such as obesity and high blood pressure, would not unduly influence the outcome.

The researchers found that the heart attack victims had worked significantly longer hours and slept less than the men who had no coronary events. They also determined that getting no more than five hours sleep for just two nights a week doubled or even tripled the risk of a heart attack.

Reflections: Exercise 2

Now that you have your to-do lists prioritized, what obstacles do you foresee? What steps can you take to overcome these obstacles?

_____

_____

_____

_____

_____

_____

What have you decided to do to reclaim your health? Will you begin by walking? Taking up a sport? Eating healthier? Is there someone who might do this with you?

_____

_____

_____

_____

What creative outlets do you have? If you do not have one yet, what do you see yourself taking up? How can you get started? Is there anyone who might start the process along with you?

_____

_____

_____

_____

What have you always wanted to learn? Have you ever wanted to advance your education? Obtain a higher degree?

_____

_____

_____

_____

Exercise 3

Detach From Control

*How having an unemotional attitude toward your job
can protect your personal power and turn you into a peak performer*

Summary

1. Recognize that you may have symptoms of stress caused by someone at work trying to use fear as a means of controlling you, and refuse to allow yourself to be emotionally sucked into their control dramas.

2. Understand how fear of termination can pressure you into a syndrome of overwork at the expense of your sleep, exercise, family concerns and your mission.

3. Take positive steps to detach yourself emotionally from such control, by:

    ● refusing to take control dramas personally.

    ● defining the terms of your employment and your own performance criteria.

    ● dealing with situations honestly and frankly.

    ● keeping everything that happens in perspective.

4. Make a point of not allowing yourself to be drawn into an emotional or angry confrontation with a controlling or counterproductive superior.

*"... if it is a care you would cast off, that care has been chosen by
you rather than imposed upon you. And if it is a fear you would
dispel, the seat of that fear is in your heart and not in the hand of
the feared."*
— *Kahlil Gibran*

Is a repetitive cycle of stress, sleepless nights, and anxiety putting
you into a funk? Do you wonder why you never seem to feel rested?
Before you start asking your doctor for one of those calming prescription
drugs advertised on TV, you might want to give some thought to what's
causing you to feel that way. Could the source of your problems be a
series of control dramas that have been inflicted on you by your boss or
the faceless corporate culture in which you work? Many times, such
"control-drama stress" can feel like a low-level headache or a "cloud of
muck that just won't seem to go away."

To eliminate it, the first thing you have to do is face up to the reality
that someone is attempting to control you and that you are in a "cloud
of muck." Most of us do not want to admit this. Even though we may
be aware of it on a subliminal level, it's not the type of thing we want
to acknowledge could happen to us (especially since we know we will
be going back there tomorrow). But once you do, you can begin to
detach by stepping back and asking yourself whether this drama has any
relevance to your personal mission (or, for that matter, the company's),
or is merely being used to distract your attention from what's really
important in your life. Ask yourself what purpose the manipulation is
serving, what sort of agenda is involved, and who is actually driving it.
Is this all part of an attempt to keep you and others under the corporation's
thumb, or does it evolve from a superior's insecurity (which is where I find
most such control dramas originate)? In other words, what is the real truth
behind the scenes?

Realizing that such control and fear tactics are consistent with neither
your own mission nor that of the company can make their meaningful-
ness begin to slowly dissolve. Becoming aware of the true nature of
the situation and the effect it is having on your ability to pursue your
mission and your vision is your best weapon for immediately neutralizing
control. In fact, you may well be able to predict what kind of control
dramas to expect and insulate yourself from them in advance.

An understanding of how control scenarios stem from either the
insecurities of peers or superiors or their hidden agendas will help you
lose the fear that would-be controllers try to instill in you. And when
you've managed to successfully detach yourself from their influence,

you may well find that you'll be able to sleep a lot more soundly—and feel a lot better. You might even discover how amusing such control dramas really are. As a board member of a company for which I once worked told me, "Anthony, your job is to be aloof—to lighten up the team by having some fun."

The corporate control drama as Oscar-winning comedy

It's hard to accomplish your mission or live up to your vision, if corporate control and coercion have turned you into someone other than who you really are, acting out other people's agendas and adopting values that are alien to your nature. I believe this happens to most of us. It can be very difficult to address when you need a regular paycheck and will be going back to the same place the next day. But facing up to the situation is the first step in achieving emotional detachment from it.

Over 40 years ago, legendary screenwriter/director Billy Wilder tackled the subject of such manipulation by corporate executives in an insightful dramatic comedy, *The Apartment*. This film classic, which won five Oscars including best picture, starred Jack Lemmon as C.C. Baxter, a white-collar drone working for a large New York City insurance firm, where his complicity with company bigwigs enables him to rise rapidly through the ranks. The key to his getting ahead is the key to his midtown apartment, which he allows the higher-ups to use for extra-marital trysts. Complications arise, however, when the woman he secretly adores (Shirley MacLaine), devastated by the realization that Baxter's philandering boss Sheldrake is simply using her, swallows a bottle of sleeping pills she finds there. She's rescued just in time by Baxter and his neighbor, a Jewish doctor who thinks Baxter responsible and advises him to become a "mensch"—that is, "a human being" (or, as the dictionary defines it, an individual who's "good, kind, decent and honorable"). But Sheldrake rewards Baxter with a further promotion and a posh office on the 27th floor, along with all the perks reserved for top management.

The stage is thus set for an unforgettable scene, in which Sheldrake again asks Baxter for the key to the apartment, confiding that he intends to go there on New Year's Eve with the same girl. "Sorry Mr. Sheldrake," Baxter replies. "You're not going to bring anybody to my apartment—especially Miss Kubelik."

Taken aback by such insubordination, Sheldrake reminds his underling that "normally, it takes years to work your way up to the 27th floor—but it only takes 30 seconds to be out on the street again. You dig?"

"I dig," says Baxter, and hands him the key. Only it turns out to be the key to the executive washroom, which Baxter tells his boss he won't be needing any more. "Just following doctor's orders," he says. "I've decided to become a mensch." He then walks out on his privileged position—but ends up getting the girl, who runs back to him after being won over by his moral courage.

While much has changed since that picture was made, the temptation for superiors to use fear as a motivation remains as firmly entrenched as ever. They may be less blatant or unscrupulous (although not always) than those depicted in the film. You probably won't be expected, for instance, to give your bosses access to your apartment. What they may attempt to coerce you into doing, however, is to make yourself accessible at all times for whatever might suit the company's—or their own—convenience or objectives. But, remember, you're there to do a job with specific performance objectives—and whatever that job is, it shouldn't mean having to sell out either your personal goals, your integrity, or your ability to accomplish your personal mission. You have already taken steps to prevent them from taking control of your existence and sucking you into their value system. The two previous exercises—formulating your personal mission and reclaiming the time that belongs to you—should already have gotten you started on erecting a barrier to anyone intruding into your space with an agenda different from yours.

Remember—the corporation, by its very nature, is subject to control dramas. Anyone drawing an organizational chart can see that there is only one box at the top and that the boxes beneath it are each linked to more and more boxes in cascading fashion until you have a "power pyramid." In the majority of companies, I believe that most of those boxes are occupied by honest, dedicated, hard-working individuals. But it only takes one insecure superior or peer to create undue stress on those below by creating control dramas. It's so easy to get caught up in them, as they are such an inherent part of the corporate culture. The problem arises when you respond by doing things out of fear that are inconsistent with your inclinations and counterproductive to your mission. Such a reaction affects every cell of your being, causing your immune system to flare up just as it would to an invasion of bacteria. With your body working so hard to try and restore its balance, you are going to feel about as well as when you're fighting off an illness. This 'fear hangover' doesn't benefit anyone—not you, your family nor the company you work for.

The pressure pump that's used to inflate earnings—and stock prices

Like all potentially manipulative entities, the corporate culture has various strategies for persuading employees to voluntarily relinquish their power. Control issues include (but are not limited to) dress codes, constant conferences, meeting upon meeting, follow-up upon follow-up and an overriding sense that you are being continually watched (even in such things as when your car enters and leaves the parking lot) and evaluated on, among other things, how much of a "team player" you are. But whereas in sports, being a team player means being willing to do whatever is in the best interest of the team, in business it all too often means being little more than a sycophant to an insecure superior—one whose own sense of insecurity is apt to be both amplified by pressure from above and used by the superior to instill fear in underlings. And in the typical corporate structure—or what's called the corporate command and control model—all the power, all the decision-making emanates down from the top to the bottom. The assumption, of course, is that no one but the person at the very top knows how to do things the right way (the "I-know-better-than-you" syndrome). Like the Light Brigade in Alfred Lord Tennyson's famous poem, yours is not to reason why, but simply to do or die. And that approach, unfortunately, is what has recently caused a number of U.S. business behemoths to ride—or rather, slide—into the valley of debt and debacle. Even more significantly, it is costing U.S. industry approximately $300 billion per year in absenteeism, health problems and programs to help stressed-out (or burnt-out) workers.

CEOs don't operate in a vacuum. They face a difficult challenge in today's publicly-owned company. Whether they like it or not, their corporate mission has tended more and more toward a single, overriding objective—the generation of short-term earnings that inflate the value of company stock, often by whatever means seems most expedient at the time. This is a difficult truth for most of us to admit. And while an admittedly small percentage of companies have recently been caught cheating—indulging in a variety of accounting tricks—that is not what is impacting most corporate employees. Inside the corporate culture itself there has been a widespread effect of squeezing the employees wherever and whenever possible—whether it be through budget cuts, increased performance or sales quotas, or, as discussed in the previous chapter, demands that people give up their evenings or weekends by working long hours of overtime, whether paid or unpaid (often by simply requiring one person to do the job of two or three). This creates fear, which then exponentially triggers control-drama-induced stress at all levels of the organization. Thus has the standard nine-to-five work week increasingly evolved into an eight-to-seven work week. And if you think you're being overtaxed—hey, welcome to the club of equal opportunity exploitation. Or, as a long-term employee asked the team at a meeting I recently attended, "When did we stop having fun?" All of which helps explain why "stress is increasing dramatically," to quote Dr. Paul Rosch, president of the American Institute of Stress (AIS), who estimates that a million workers are absent daily due to its effects.

This bottom-line-over-all orientation tends to become particularly pronounced following corporate mergers and takeovers, which have become all too routine in today's dehumanized economic climate. In such situations, many people's jobs are apt to be deemed redundant, resulting in staff reductions—or the new owners may simply decide to cut costs by eliminating people in essential positions and expecting coworkers to fill the void. Either way, employees tend to find themselves saddled with extra responsibilities and pressures. Most merger and acquisition deals that I have studied are built around such consolidation and low-cost operating budgets. I have mixed emotions about these arrangements. Handled properly, I believe most are done in an ethical way, with employees treated fairly. In any event, consolidation to streamline operations in today's market is going to happen no matter what.

Typical of this syndrome is what happened when a large and lucrative family-owned newspaper was purchased by one of the country's leading publicly-owned chains. Although assurances had been made to employees that their jobs would not be affected, the new publisher sent in by the company immediately began slashing what he saw as all unnecessary expenditures—including those for personnel. As an ex-employee recalls, besides eliminating things like the budget for freelance contributions and courtesy coffee for people working the night shift, his first orders of business included summarily dismissing a whole contingent of editors who worked on an as-needed basis—abolishing in one night a highly effective arrangement that the paper had relied on for many years to accommodate fluctuating workloads. Not only did this abrupt down-sizing serve to demoralize the staff, it also placed an added burden on the already strained full-time people who remained. (But then, the new publisher had clearly been sent there to do whatever it took to cut expenditures and maximize profits, something he did so well that he was soon put in charge of the chain's entire statewide operation.)

Many corporate "roll-up" strategies—buying up companies and eliminating overhead—are now proving to be failures, as in the case of Tyco, which, rather than building a company with a base culture (from the ground up), attempted to merge several existing companies. Lou

Gerstner Jr., chairman of IBM, said it best: "If life was so easy that you could just go buy success, there would be a lot more successful companies in the world. Successful enterprises are built from the ground up. You can't assemble them from a bunch of acquisitions."

Whatever the why and wherefore, when interviewing people for this book I was amazed at how insecure managers have a whole bag of psychological tricks for getting people to go above and beyond the call of duty in order to help maximize reported earnings and stock prices. A technique used by one major insurance company, for instance, was to e-mail employees at 2 or 3 a.m., the idea being that if the boss is pulling all-nighters, so should you. (A variant of this technique is to leave a phone message that begins with something like "It's 4 in the morning, and I'm still here.") Or you might be made to feel that by failing to put in those extra hours, you're somehow letting your coworkers down (or not being a "team player")—almost as if you're all soldiers in a combat situation (hard to believe, but true, as I discovered in interviews with several different-level managers at a large insurance company).

Although meetings serve an important purpose in getting multiple tasks accomplished, as well as allowing people to get to know one another, they can also be "control dramas." Perpetual meetings may be used as a tool for keeping employees under management's thumb. The members of one corporate group with whom I worked, for example, were expected to attend a management meeting every other week. In one such session, a manager who had particularly impressed me with his efficiency at running 26 different operations posed the question: "Who benefits from these meetings?" It was easy to see that the query had made the CEO and other staff members rather uncomfortable, but finally the CEO blurted out, "I need these meetings to keep you guys coordinated." What he was really saying was he needed the meetings to make sure he retained control and influence over the management group. Interestingly enough, at this same meeting the CEO admitted that he had the least number of concerns and issues with that particular department—but it didn't keep him from tying it up in a continual, time-consuming meeting syndrome.

The kind of meeting where the agenda is long and the objective is to move through it quickly is also a very typical control drama. One controlling CEO I know measures the quality of a meeting by its speed and the absence of an opposing viewpoint. And guess what? The participants are all sure to accommodate him! They have the "actual" meeting afterward, voicing their gripes and wasting real time and productivity, just to oblige the CEO's sense of being in control.

Objective honesty: an antidote for the fear of being fired

Underlying most corporate control dramas is the unspoken fear of being fired. In fact, you've set the stage for one as soon as you think of having to go without a regular paycheck, and the way this might affect your family and responsibilities. Fear of termination is the most powerful lever the corporation has for keeping you in line. One major corporation with whom I was affiliated early in my career paid married people a higher wage. In fact, during personnel reviews it was common to check that box, the thinking being that matrimony would make for a more responsible employee—or one more fearful of being terminated.

Admittedly, living in such fundamental dread isn't an easy state from which to free yourself—especially if you haven't allowed yourself to recognize that you are enmeshed in it. As a story from the Reuters business wire recently noted, "Fears of losing jobs as the economy stalls or not having a personal life as pagers, cell phones, and the Internet keep employees linked to their work 24 hours/day have Americans complaining of muscular pain or fatigue or else seeking therapy."[3] But, unless you're holding that winning lottery ticket or have just come into a sizable inheritance, it's almost impossible to shed this dread without cultivating a certain aura of detachment.

The key to detachment is to focus on the fact that this drama is not you, nor is it consistent with your mission—and to step back and look at it for what it is: someone else's agenda, someone else's issue, someone else's insecurity. Don't let their fears become yours. Once you've done that, it enables you to deal with a controlling individual honestly, objectively, dispassionately, and with a certain protective layer of self-confidence. You'll thus be in a better position to confront the "controller" on a one-on-one basis and to be sensitive to his or her own insecurities because you'll have stopped taking the way you're being treated personally. It is critically important that you do not deal with the individual's insecurity in an emotional way yourself. If you allow yourself to get angry, you are in effect giving that person your power, and the negative emotions of anger and fear will cause your body to mount a defensive response. When someone gets defensive and lets their emotions get the best of them, things can culminate in open displays of anger that can result in people getting fired if for no other reason than to allow the manager involved to save face. This is the ultimate loss of power and the maximum impact of fear. But if you respond to the person's insecurity by asking— perhaps just in your manner—"How can I help you," your body will become more relaxed and so will the individual you are confronting, likely ending this particular control drama game. When you recognize underlying insecurity in the individual and empathize with it, the power shifts back to you. You will immediately feel better and when you convey to the insecure person that you are not a threat, in most cases, they will back off as well. Remember, though, you have to emotionally detach from the situation—completely. In fact, as long as you keep things private and unemotional, being candid and truthful with the person trying to control you will actually strengthen your position.

Of course, there are always exceptions to the above-mentioned rule of control-drama resolution through detachment. Some people—particularly those involved in financial shenanigans—may prefer to get rid of employees who lay it on the line, or refuse to go along with some managerial agenda, as C.C. Baxter's boss in *The Apartment* was quick to remind him, and as I myself have recently discovered. If that's the kind of situation in which you find yourself, it is better to keep your mouth shut, detach, and get your resume out. (In fact, it's quite possible for a corporate merger or buyout to corrupt the climate of the organization, even if it wasn't that way originally. In that case, the faster you detach from any emotional connection to the job and look for employment elsewhere, the better off you'll be. This is one of the reasons why maintaining the kind of "people options" discussed further on in Exercise 5 can be essential to your survival.

Strategies for avoiding enslavement to short-term earnings mania

To keep from being sucked into the perpetual performance machine that so many companies are now utilizing to pump up short-term earnings, it's necessary to see it for what it is—and not to allow yourself to be fooled into believing that it's really something else.

For instance, make sure the heroic effort to "save the company" (and presumably, your job) from going under is real. (In way too many cases, it may be your boss's job, his bonus—or even his/her boss's position—that's actually in jeopardy.) That's not to say that firms aren't occasionally placed in precarious straits, especially in our capricious economy—but if that's your employer's situation, chances are you'll have heard something about it, either through the grapevine or more official channels. (My own experience says that many times the grapevine is more honest, straightforward and accurate than the manager leading a department) A far more likely explanation for your being asked to comply with extraordinary demands is simply pressure from above to maximize those quarterly profits and inflate stock values. In most cases, if this is a short-term situation with no hidden agendas and everybody involved being up-front and honest, it can actually be challenging, fun and rewarding. But if there are other motivations and this becomes a long-term proposition with no letup, it can prove problematic by taking time away from your personal mission, family and fitness program, jeopardizing your health in the process.

And, yes, giving in to corporate pressure on a routine basis or for an extensive period of time is putting your health at risk. For one thing, relinquishing control of your life and putting yourself under that kind of pressure is bound to create stress on your vital organs, making you a candidate for an eventual heart attack or some other serious affliction if it continues for a period of longer than three months. The very phenomenon of this type of fear-based control, in fact, tends to be toxic in itself. Controlling individuals can have the same toxic effect as pesticides in food, and you should do everything you can to avoid such people. They're the ones, for example, who demand so much of your personal time, it's likely to be keeping you from getting the exercise you need to maintain good health (as was detailed in the previous chapter). Ultimately, it's apt to be causing you to cut down on sleep—and there's simply no substitute for a full night's sleep, as so many medical experts have lately emphasized. In short, acceptance of exploitation is a very unhealthy attitude that can be literally toxic—and it is you who is making the choice to surrender your power.

Perhaps you've chosen to do so because you think the continuation of that all-important paycheck depends on it. But think about this: when you are in this state, you are not apt to be productive, innovative or feeling good—and that's not the result the company is looking for. What the company wants is peak performance—and the only way you can be in a position to deliver it is to emotionally detach from this fear-based control and speak up. Let them know you need time to exercise and to sleep. You can't afford to wait for permission or support from others to stand up for your rights. If fitness training or family commitments are important, make sure that key people know and respect that. I am reminded of one particular meeting at which our management group was trying to impress a new CEO. When the meeting had dragged on for hours going into overtime, I finally arose, with some trepidation, and announced I would really have to leave. I let the executive vice president know on the way out that I had an appointment with my personal trainer at 5:30 and didn't intend to miss it. Later, the CEO took the group by surprise when he told them I was someone who had his priorities straight.

Methods of detaching

Once having realized the nature of attempts to control and coerce you and the kind of harm that can result, you've ready to take steps to make your emotional, psychological and spiritual escape. Here are some detachment strategies I recommend.

1. Stay true to your personal mission.

Step away and look at yourself in the mirror from a distance, squinting a bit so everything appears somewhat blurred. Then ask yourself, 'Is what I'm doing consistent with either my mission or that of the company, or is my attention being diverted by irrelevant concerns?'

2. Quit taking it personally.

Come to the realization that whatever the situation at your office, it most likely stems from someone else's agenda and insecurities, and that emotionally detaching from it is the best way to deal with it.

3. Establish your own 'performance criteria' and rules of employment.

Define in your mind the terms of your employment as you understand them, what's expected of you, what you expect in return, and establish the limits of that arrangement. Then make a mental recording of this "contract."

4. Make sure you are rested and feeling good.

That's when you're able to achieve peak performance, which is what the company is looking for. So don't be shy about speaking up when you feel you're being deprived of necessary rest or exercise. If you do, you'll command respect. If you don't, your own insecurity will make you ripe for control.

5. Recognize attempts at control and use them to benefit you.

When you're working for controlling individuals, be aware of it and use it to your advantage whenever possible by letting them, in effect, do most of your work for you. Don't worry if what they want seems like the wrong approach or isn't up to your standards—remember, it's their issue, not yours (something we'll touch on at greater length in the next chapter). Get your satisfaction somewhere else—from a personal mission or a creative pursuit you can control (as we discussed in the two previous chapters).

6. When you have to work over the weekend, make it on your terms.

Assess the situation for what it is—an imposition—and don't act as if this is something that's now routinely expected of you.

7. Make sure you're given accurate and realistic time frames.

Don't accept deadlines as unquestionable edicts. Controlling people love to set unreasonable deadlines.

8. Keep everything in perspective.

When stress levels start building, keep telling yourself, "This is not me—It's only a job." Ask yourself what it is you're really afraid of.

9. Be straightforward and honest with everyone.

Let it be known—politely, but firmly—how you feel about the issues involved. If nothing else, it'll win you respect, and who knows?—It may even help resolve things by dispelling the climate of timidity that helps promote inequity. Your candor, in fact, will help you become known as an individual who can be trusted. Above all, be honest with yourself. Don't rationalize any of the answers. Truth is your best armor against the slings and arrows of manipulative management.

10. View the situation as you would a situation comedy.

You'll find yourself being highly amused at the absurdity of most of the control dramas you encounter, enabling you to recognize the insecurity behind them and to actually empathize with the principal actors.

Is a hidden agenda or personal insecurity the real problem?

Controlling behavior, of course, does not always stem from insecurity. Sometimes, it's a result of the ulterior motives of individual managers. This is apt to be the case when you find yourself working under someone who seems intent on hindering progress and subverting your best efforts.

An example of that syndrome was the situation I encountered early in my career when I worked at a Fortune 200 company. I had been asked to take over the pricing department by the president of the division, a guy who liked to keep all its aspects under close control and, for all intents and purposes, ran an extremely tight ship. The department had about 30 employees whose ultimate objective was to manage the gross margin of the division on a weekly basis. For me, it was an impressive new area of responsibility, which involved working with every part of the company and every single brand and product manager, and I was determined to prove just how proficient I was at restoring the division, which had recently begun to slip, to full fiscal health.

The problem was that the president kept pushing and pushing our margins to the point where our actual market share was decreasing significantly—and this had begun to demoralize many of the people involved, from brand managers to sales people out in the field. So, in an effort to reverse the situation, I suggested to him that we get a group of brand managers and other key people together for an off-site meeting and try to come up with some alternative strategies. He said "fine," and we proceeded to do just that, getting together at a place called Innsbrook where we came up with a pretty elaborate plan that was rather bold for the time. We then asked for a meeting with the president at an off-site hotel, where we could present it to him. After looking at every sheet on our flip chart, he told us, "You know, this is good work." That was his whole response. Then he left.

As it turned out, there were changes that occurred in the aftermath of that meeting—but not the kind we had proposed. Instead, within several weeks, two of the key players in our group found themselves ostracized, another was let go, and another one was replaced and put out to pasture in a less responsible job. This served its purpose—to quickly diffuse any enthusiasm for the plan. In essence, after seeing the proposal, the president was determined to make sure that no one else got wind of it—and effectively managed to bury it by splintering the group that conceived it. That, in fact, was my rude awakening to the potential degree of control a corporate model can exercise. But it wasn't until several months after I left that I learned of the president's real rationale when a friend sent me an article from a major newspaper that told how the president had ended up with a $10 million bonus from the sale of the division—a transaction based largely on the margins that were being reported without regard to the loss in market share.

Another sort of ulterior motive is that of the "control freak" whose arbitrary demands and meddlesome tactics often seemed deliberately contrived to be counterproductive. Should you have the misfortune of being creative or innovative while working under such an individual, beware!—instead of being appreciated, your efforts are far more apt to encounter roadblocks, static and interference, and even elicit abuse. In such cases, the better and more diligent you are at your job, the more likely your superior is to perceive you as a threat—and thus try to find ways of sabotaging you and attempting to keep you in your place. If you recognize it for what it is, it's much easier to deal with. And remember: these control dramas are about them, not you. The issues involved are their issues, not yours. Dealing with them straight on is only possible when you detach emotionally.

Keeping a sabotaging superior from getting to you

What's the best way to cope with a self-serving boss who's a counter-productive control freak? Having to deal with a situation of this sort, after all, isn't quite the same as simply being pressured by an underlying bottom-line-driven culture, since it involves someone who's determined to keep you from putting forth your best effort to benefit the company.

There are some tactical defenses you can use when up against such a manipulative individual. Once it's clear to you that your work is being deliberately sabotaged, and you thoroughly understand the insecurity and the motive, you might, depending on circumstances, attempt to have yourself transferred out of that person's domain—perhaps citing philosophical differences, if you don't want to rock the boat—or, if things get really ugly, petition a higher-up in the company to arbitrate matters. But those aren't always viable avenues (especially when the person you're dealing with is the CEO). If the previous steps don't work and the abuse becomes blatant, you should stand up to the source directly and ask why.

But never let your emotion in such a situation turn to anger or let the person bait you into a confrontation, for you will lose every time. Keep it firmly in mind that unfair or unwarranted attacks in the presence of others are deliberately contrived to provoke you—and give the person ammunition to use against you. The fact that you will always lose such exchanges enables your superior to obscure the actual issue involved and instead make an issue about your "unprofessional "attitude. It's essential that you not assist this person in building such a case and do whatever you can do to avoid a confrontation.

What's most important in this type of situation, however, is for you to thoroughly *detach* psychologically. That's not always easy, of course, when someone is attempting to demean you or using various devices to intimidate you. But if you let them get inside of you, you're bound to suffer a toxic reaction—and when that happens, in a way you've let them win. Remember, no one can hurt you in this manner without your giving them permission. When you emotionally detach and recognize their insecurity, whatever they do just bounces off your back. In the meantime, start taking whatever steps are necessary to physically distance yourself from them as well. In other words, do not give your power up to anyone—it's still your power, after all, and your choice.

As for people screwing up your ability to do your job—whether for mercenary motives, like the president I mentioned, or simply because they perceive you as a threat—there are ways for coping with that, too. If you are 'on mission,' striving to attain your vision, taking care of yourself, and making an honest, truthful assessment of your company's culture and your boss's attitude, you're already well ahead of the game. If you can only learn to separate yourself from the individual's desired outcome, you'll be another step closer to being able to successfully survive in a command-and-control environment—with your identity and integrity intact, and in the end, being a peak performer for the company.

Controlling stress by taking control of your own life

While workplace stress and its pernicious effects have been steadily worsening due to factors like layoffs and job insecurity, there is a way you can reduce your own stress level. It's to assume control of as many things related to your work as possible—even little ones.

So says Dr. Paul Rosch, president of the American Institute of Stress, who has spent a half century researching the subject, and who believes that a person's attitude has a lot to do with how stressed they are.

"All of our clinical and laboratory research confirms that not having control is always stressful," he says. 'Numerous studies show that even little tiny things that don't seem important, just allowing people in the workplace to pick the colors of their space, arrange their furniture, provide some minimal sense of control. Feeling a sense of control is something you can learn to do." And while there is no "cook-book" formula for doing this, "people can learn to adapt to situations so that they have some sense of control over them."

First, it's important to recognize that "stress is an unavoidable consequence of the human condition" and "some stress you can do something about, some you can't. The trick is leaning to distinguish between the two." To do that, Rosch recommends making a list of all things you find stressful and categorizing them as either things you can do something about or things you can't.

"You have to look at each situation and determine whether you've exhausted your options," he says. "For example, if what should be a 15-minute commute takes you over an hour, what category would you put that in? Can you do something about that or can't you?"

You might, for instance, go to your boss and suggest that you come in an hour early and leave an hour early, or do some of your work at home. And he might well respond that if he did that for you, he'd have to do it for everybody.

What then? "Well, instead of having a miserable commute and trying to find shortcuts to and from work, you could say, 'I've done what I can—now I'm going to take this time and use it productively, maybe learn a foreign language or listen to a book I haven't had time to read. Now when you finally get to work, you want to sit in the car another five minute and listen to the end of the story. So you've turned a stressful situation into something that's semi-pleasurable. Why? Simply because you've gained some sense of control over it."

Stress, Rosch says, has nothing to do with a job per se, but rather how the individual fits into the environment at issue. "We all respond differently to the same stimuli," he notes. "What is very distressing to some people is pleasurable to others." A favorite example of his is the way different people react to being on a roller coaster. "Some will sit in the back seats with their eyes shut and their jaws clenched, while up front you have the thrill seekers." And in between, he points out, you can find those with an air of nonchalance bordering on boredom. What distinguishes these individuals from each other, he says, "is a sense of control they perceive over the event. Neither group has any more or less control, but their perceptions and expectations are quite different. That's what stress is all about.

The exit strategy—your 'ace in the hole'

While this book is designed to be a corporate survivor's manual, there are times when survival calls for nothing less than abandoning ship. And because that's always a distinct possibility, even under the best of circumstances (remember the Titanic), it never hurts to have a lifeboat at the ready and an orderly evacuation plan in mind.

For employees in extremely competitive situations, however, planning to physically detach themselves from the mother ship at the first opportunity can be a great way of emotionally detaching while staying afloat on the job. (Making plans to leave my first job after 10 years, for instance, enabled me to separate myself from it psychologically before actually doing so). If such an "exit strategy" can help you survive in your present circumstances, I say go for it!

Such was the case with an individual I'll call Ed. As Ed described it, he was in an extremely "uncomfortable environment," having to put up with "a very temperamental boss" who had "control issues"—a "my-way-or-the- highway" type of guy. Ed was working seven-day weeks in this "very suffocating" situation. After a year, it was putting him into a funk. "I was not a happy person," he recalled. "I was trying to figure out, 'What do I do? How do I change this?' My boss would talk to me in a tone that made me feel like I was in first grade." So condescending did Ed find this attitude, in fact, that rather than consulting with the boss, he would simply try to figure everything out on his own. "If I were to call him up and ask any question, I would get a 15-minute dressing down, again as if I were six years old." So Ed just started working through other channels to help get the information he needed. But Ed's frustration was building to the point where he resolved to quit. Fortunately, he had readied a "lifeboat" in the form of both savings and a web of contacts. He also noted, "My wife and I don't live beyond our means. Therefore, I could go without a paycheck for a while. That empowered me to make my decision."

So one day—a Monday before Thanksgiving—he just decided he had had enough of the aggravation, the patronizing treatment, and waking up every morning with a negative outlook. It happened when he was called into his boss's office to face a typical tirade. "What are you going to do to fix this?" the boss demanded, to which Ed responded "I'll tell you exactly what I'm going to do. I quit."

Suddenly the boss's whole demeanor changed. "What can we do to help you?" he asked.

"The decision has been made," Ed replied. "I'm just not going to take it any more. My health is going downhill, my outlook on life sucks right now, and it can all be traced back to what I have to deal with here every day. This isn't a fun place to be." With that, he walked out, drove home, and, as he explained, "when I got out of the car, I felt like this tremendous weight had been lifted from my shoulders. I was just elated." And then I thought, "Now, what?" But something told me this will work out for the better." And it did. After taking some time off to "get grounded," his phone rang and "kept ringing with people saying they needed help on this project, that project. Now I'm working with people that I truly enjoy being around every day."

In Ed's "exit interview," he was told, "Nobody quits this company. It's growing so well and you get stock options"—again, holding out money as an incentive to stay.

Ed's advice to others in the company: sit down and just start putting together an exit strategy. Figure out the amount of money you spend on peripheral things that you don't need. If you were to put that money into your 'rainbow pot,' a year from now you might have enough money to get out.

While I certainly am not recommending this course of action—it's admittedly risky, and something that you have to be quite sure in your own mind that you're ready for—Ed's story illustrates just how much power some of us have that we are unaware of until we've gotten up the courage to completely detach.

Perhaps an even more dramatic example of that phenomenon was the bold decision made a number of years ago by an advertising executive

I'll call Phil. He had left an ad agency that he liked, but in which he was not advancing, for a position with a competitive company that was supposedly about to land a big fast-food account that Phil had been promised he'd be put in charge of. But Instead, upon arriving at his new job, he was immediately shuttled off to take charge of a shoe manufacturing account, even though he didn't know the first thing about fashion advertising. To make matters worse, Bob, the client's advertising manager turned out be a controlling egomaniac who told Phil, "Let's be clear up front— I don't get ulcers, I give ulcers," and proceeded to belittle everything the agency did as "hopelessly incompetent."

"In that first meeting, my life began to flash before my eyes," is how Phil described it. "I had quit a great job at a great agency with great clients who loved me to come to work for this jerk. I had a wife and two babies at home, there was a recession on, and jobs were scarce. What was I going to do?"

What Phil did was to immediately begin to detach from the man's control. "Interestingly, as the abuse wore on I began to get some distance from it," he recollected. He also took notes on this behavior, helping him to cope.

In the last meeting between the two, Bob delivered another of his verbal tirades, then glared across his desk at Phil and demanded, "So what are you going to do now?" To which Phil replied, "Well Bob, what I'm going to do is take all of my notes on all of your comments and write them up for my replacement."

Now Bob was taken aback. "What do you mean, your replacement?"

Phil responded that he had never been so humiliated in his life, and wasn't going to stand for it. So he had decided to resign, effective the next day, when he arrived back at his regional office.

"And then a funny thing happened. Bob's jaw dropped. He rose from his chair and demanded, "Wait, you can't go!" he then followed Phil down the hall, saying, "Now hold on there." He even insisted on driving Phil to the airport. But Phil would have none of it. "As the plane was boarding," he said, "I shook his hand, saying simply, 'Good-bye, Bob.'" The power had shifted to Phil.

When he arrived home, explained his decision to his wife and found her totally supportive, Phil sat down, wrote his letter of resignation and gave it to the office manager, who, instead of getting mad, was elated. "Now we have him," he crowed. "With this, I can get Bob fired. His boss will have him hog-tied for this. You did great!"

"But I still quit," Phil said. "This is my two weeks' notice." The office manager appeared flabbergasted, and reminded Phil about the fast-food account. But Phil replied he didn't believe there would be such an account, and didn't think he needed to be there.

Now comes the part that makes this story read like an improbable movie script. The very next day, Phil got a call from his old boss, asking how the new job was going. Not revealing his hand, Phil replied that it had some good aspects and some bad ones. The two then agreed to meet for lunch, during which Phil's old boss described how unhappy the client was with his having left. Was there a chance he might reconsider? Phil indicated there was—but he'd have to get a much better deal this time. And that's what he ended up getting—returning to his original agency with an improved status, and with his "time off" treated as an unpaid leave.

Again, while I'm not recommending that anyone follow Phil's example, he is living proof of the power of detaching from control. Once he started to write the notes for his replacement, the power shifted back to him.

How CEOs came up—and got their 'comeuppance'

If too many of today's CEOs seem driven by short-term share-holder interests, that wasn't always the case. In a special issue of *Fortune* magazine devoted to "The CEO Under Fire," Reginald Jones, the former CEO of General Electric, was quoted from an interview he gave shortly after he retired in 1981 as saying that "too many managers feel under pressure to concentrate on the short term in order to satisfy the financial community and the owners of the enterprise—the stockholders. Boards of directors have to understand that they must shelter management from these pressures. They should do it in the interest of the nation."

But as writer Jerry Useem observed, delivering shareholder value soon became the primary mission of CEOs, with stock options used to get managers to go along. Soon, "CEOs began taking options grants worth … tens and even hundreds of millions" Thus "instead of treating the stock price as the natural byproduct of building a successful company, they began pursuing it as an end in itself, boosting their own net worth but often crippling the company's long-term prospects in the process."

The article goes on to interpret the survival of "the imperial CEO "as being based on a fact observed as far back as 1932—that shareholders and board members didn't come to the office every day. "That left the CEO with a chokehold on information and, therefore a position as the ultimate advantaged insider."[4]

Confronting an out-of-control CEO

At what point is it time for a showdown between a management team and a "in-control" CEO who has clearly gotten out of control (otherwise known as "CEO Disease")—and how should such a confrontation be conducted?

Unfortunately, there are no pat answers. But when the CEO's enlarged ego and heavy-handed tactics reach the point of having placed everyone else in a "why bother?" mode that may be sufficient cause to challenge his or her authority—provided you've got a consensus that favors doing so. In other words, first make sure the entire team agrees there's a problem with the CEO that needs to be addressed.

Secondly, make sure this is not an "ambush," but rather an attempt to deal with someone who, like a substance abuser, is in denial. Talk out the specific issues, eliminate all emotional responses, and make sure everyone has a positive approach and outcome in mind for the CEO. Perhaps this command-and-control "pace setter" can't be turned into a visionary, but can be turned into a collaborator. And collaboration, listening to and engaging the management team can be the first step toward a "cure" for CEO Disease.

It's essential to know what your purpose is. Remember that many of the senior managers may be at an age where they cannot easily find another job, and may be reluctant to stand up to the CEO. One way to assure that everyone stands together is to get a commitment from each participant that should anyone be singled out and fired, then everyone tenders his or her resignation.

Despite all such precautions, I can offer no guarantees that such a confrontation will be successful—in fact, it could prove to be a very difficult situation for everyone involved. But even if it proves totally ineffective, if the management group presents enough of a united front, at the very least its members will have established a great bond with each other as "stand-up" individuals who refused to surrender their integrity to corporate domination.

The protocol for handling this type of situation is always first to address the individual directly. If that doesn't work, the next person the problem should be taken up with is the chairman of the board (although I have seen very few of these situations reach the board level with any success.) In today's companies, audit governance committees are much more active than they have ever been and may also be approached.

Now get ready for a whole new perspective on results

With your personal power restored, life will start to look brighter. To review, you have formulated both a personal mission and a vision that you are taking steps toward realizing, and are reclaiming the time that belongs to you for keeping fit, cultivating your special skills and interests, and family life. You've also come to recognize the insecurities or ulterior motives of people who engineer control dramas at work, and refusing to let them involve you in their farce any longer. Next, you'll learn to detach emotionally from whatever results you achieve on your job—be they positive or negative—and focus your feelings on the things, like your personal mission, that really matter in your life.

Reflections: Exercise 3

Make a list of "stressors" at your job. Be as specific as possible. If it is a person whose control dramas get to you, write down specific actions of that person. Include anything from the tiniest stressors to job-threatening ones.

_____

_____

_____

Which of the above daily stressors can you eliminate through emotional detachment?

_____

_____

_____

Jot down a "worst case scenario" at your job. Step back and think of a reaction—one different than one you might have had in the past. How is this new reaction different than a previous one? What different results can you predict?

_____

_____

_____

Reread your job description. (If there is not one in writing for your job, write one for yourself.) Determine the most important aspects of your job, the ones you were hired to perform, and write them below. Post them somewhere you can see them on a daily basis.

_____

_____

_____

_____

_____

Exercise 4

Detach From Results

*How to keep from confusing the 'numbers game'
with what really counts*

Summary

1. Be aware that company performance expectations don't necessarily reflect realistic goals or conditions, but may well be calculated to inflate short-term earnings or accomplish other hidden agendas.

2. Neither take failure to heart nor let success go to your head. Realize that the company numbers you're supposed to achieve are not really who "you" are, but are likely to be a reflection of someone else's agenda.

3. It's great to take pride in and satisfaction from your work— as long as it's not your principal (or only) source of pride and satisfaction. Take steps to avoid 'being the company' by reminding yourself of your mission and vision.

4. Think about business results objectively. Consider the unemotional way a consultant would react in contrast to the typical employee response.

5. Learn to view failure as a learning experience that can serve as a building block to success.

"We haven't failed. We now know a thousand things that won't work, so we are much closer to finding what will."
— *Thomas Edison*

Who or what really defines success of failure? My most notable successes, for instance, were born out of apparent failures. But then, what we view as failure may simply be our inability to measure up to either our own or someone else's unrealistic performance expectations. By the same token, what seems to be success can also be a misreading of results. Was it really you who succeeded, or were you simply fortunate enough to have ridden a mass movement that took you there?

Have you ever gone home depressed and disappointed because your company or division didn't meet its quarterly number? Try stepping back and looking at this objectively. How much impact did you really have on those results? Even more important, how will this day impact your mission over the next 10 years? Was it worth putting yourself in a foul mood? What about the negative ripple effect it may have had on your family, friends and business associates?

Corporations, of course, by their very structure hold their employees accountable for success or failure in the "numbers game." Holding a person accountable may be the right thing to do when that individual is directly responsible—for example, a budget for which you are personally responsible. In fact, when an organization does not require some measure of personal accountability, the result is a dysfunctional system. What I am referring to is an internally generated "bogey" result or "number" that many people in the organization have a piece of and that may or may not be achievable. In other words, there is very little you can personally do to impact the result. Therefore, if you do not reach it you should not be emotionally upset by it.

The bottom line in all this is quarterly EPS—earnings per share—and yearly EBITDA—earnings before interest, taxes, depreciation, and amortization. These quarterly benchmarks are just numbers. Unless you are the CEO, you should not have an emotional attachment to these numbers. That's precisely why I've chosen to devote a separate exercise to detachment from such results—because they can be a major source of frustration stemming from a sense of helplessness, and lead to the ultimate paradox, poor performance in your job and unhappiness at home. It need not be this way, of course, as in many instances apparent failure can be a springboard to fortune. But if you're tired, depressed and emotionally skewered by such immediate and transient results, you may not realize it.

Successful failures who exemplify
how the numbers don't always add up

"If you can meet with triumph and disaster
And treat these two impostors just the same…"
   — *Rudyard Kipling*

Perhaps you're familiar with the following stories—particularly the first one, which has become a sort of business legend. But I can think of no better examples of the point I'd like to emphasize.

Conventional wisdom would say when you're 66 and going out of business, it's a little late in life to be starting over. At that age, after having been forced to auction off a once thriving restaurant operation in order to pay off debts, it would probably make sense to throw in the towel and retire on one's Social Security benefits. But Harlan Sanders didn't seem to know when it was time to call it quits. The fact that he had already reached retirement age when a sharp decline in patronage, due largely to the building of a new Interstate highway, had forced him to close up shop didn't faze him in the slightest. Instead of opting to live sensibly on his monthly government checks (which in 1956 came to $105), he decided to use that supposed retirement money to pay for car trips that he and his wife would make around the country, franchising the chicken recipe he had spent years perfecting to restaurant owners. "Lots of nights I would sleep in the back of my car so I would have enough money to buy cookers the next day if someone took a franchise,' he later recalled. Along the way, he also showed eatery operators ways to improve the quality of their food.

Eight years and more than 600 franchises later, Colonel Sanders sold the rights to his Kentucky Fried Chicken enterprise to a group of investors (among them the ex-governor who had bestowed the rank on him) for $2 million.

Henry David Thoreau's mission in life may have been a far cry from Harlan Sanders'. But Thoreau, as previously noted, was someone who didn't allow himself to be put off by ostensible indicators of failure—in his case, book sales figures that couldn't have been much lower. Had he been affected by them, his first crack at getting a book published might very well have been his last, and the generations that followed him would probably never have had the benefit of being able to share the vision he communicated in his acknowledged masterpiece *Walden*. What those numbers quite clearly indicated was that few people were apparently interested in what he had to say. It was something he couldn't help but be aware of, because having failed to find a publisher for

A Week on the Concord and Merrimack Rivers (a book that included various essays and observations on a wide range of topics) he had opted to pay for the publication of 1,000 copies himself. However, only 214 of these were actually sold over a four-year period. When the publisher finally returned the remaining ones to Thoreau, he noted with characteristic good humor in his diary, "I have now a library of nearly nine hundred volumes, over seven hundred of which I wrote myself."

Walden, in fact, fared only slightly better during the eight years between its publication and the author's death in 1862, there having been no apparent reason to exceed its initial press run of 2,000 copies. Had these figures alone been the standard by which his degree of success was measured, he plainly wouldn't have been a contender in the literary world. Fortunately, it was his vision—and mission—that moved Thoreau to go on writing, not the returns on his literary efforts. Those "numbers," as it turned out, had absolutely no bearing on his true stature or significance in the literary landscape—or on the immeasurable value of his contributions to human thought.

Then there was George Washington, who suffered one defeat after another in the early stages of the American Revolution—first losing New York City, then the Battle of the Brandywine, then Philadelphia to the British. With an army in tatters after having sustained continual and heavy losses against a well-equipped and formidable enemy, another commander might well have concluded that the cause was lost and that surrender was the only viable option. Instead, Washington took the offensive, using a strategy of surprise when his forces had been all but marginalized—and went on to deliver the colonies from British occupation.

Nor should we neglect to mention Vincent Van Gogh, who managed to sell only one of his many paintings during his short and unhappy life. Whether that contributed to the chronic depression that led to his suicide is a matter of speculation—but the point is that neither his failure to gain any degree of commercial success as an artist nor his emotional problems kept him from continuing to paint—and, ironically, the collective results of that effort are now worth untold millions of dollars.

Sanders, Thoreau, Washington and Van Gogh—four very different individuals with widely divergent temperaments, talents, life histories, and objectives. Yet each, in his own way, managed to discredit the idea that short-term results and immediate prospects are reliable indicators of one's value, success or failure. The numbers may not have been on their side, but as each ultimately demonstrated, those numbers weren't what counted in the long run.

But how does that affect you in your present situation? As an object lesson, perhaps, and a concept to keep in mind—especially if the company you work for is among those demanding immediate results and pushing today's bottom-line considerations as if there were no tomorrow (or at least, no next year).

"The practice by which CEOs offer guidance about their expected quarterly earnings performance—analysts set 'targets' based on that guidance, and then companies try to meet those targets within the penny—is an old one. But in recent years, the practice has become so enshrined in the culture of Wall Street that the men and women running public companies often think of little else. They become preoccupied with short-term "success," a mindset that can hamper or even destroy long-term performance for shareholders. I call this the tyranny of quarterly earnings. … Once you get under the domination of making the quarter—even unwittingly—you start to compromise in the gray areas of your business, that wide swath of terrain between the top and bottom lines. Perhaps you'll begin to sacrifice things (such as funding a promising research-and-development project, incremental improvements to your products, customer service, employee training, expansion into new markets, and, yes, community outreach) that are important and may be vital for your company over the long term."[5]

— Daniel Vasella,
CEO, Novartis

Distancing yourself from the vicissitudes of your job

In today's corporate climate, success is measured in terms of quarterly reports. In some unique cases, ego and greed overcome all operating parameters. It's just such a syndrome that has led to the unraveling of megafirms like Enron and Worldcom, where all manner of flimflams and shell games were used by employees to drive stock prices up to unrealistic levels set by top management. Such an orientation is a bit like a tidal wave, drowning out all other values, including integrity (both of the company itself and of its products or services).

Recently I was in a corporate strategy meeting, involving a number of managers. Various projects were being discussed. There was a creative energy flowing and those in the room were getting excited. Then in came the CEO who proceeded to tell the group, "I don't give a s___ about strategies or new products—just deliver the numbers this quarter." The effect was a real damper on the level of enthusiasm, with the prevailing sentiment (although not said) being, "Why bother? It's only about meeting the number."

Actually, it's not so much bothering that's the problem as letting yourself be bothered by factors beyond your control. Dedication and commitment to the job are fine, and certainly commendable—up to the point where a negative or disappointing outcome actually succeeds in ruffling you. By the same token, you shouldn't allow yourself to become too ecstatic over positive results, especially in typical corporate win-lose situations—even if the strategic decision that made the difference was yours. It's a good idea to keep your excitement in check, try to contain your enthusiasm, and not get too carried away. Just as it's important to emotionally detach from deliberate control dramas, it's also essential to your feelings of self-confidence, self-worth and well-being that you emotionally detach yourself from whatever successes or failures you encounter in the corporate world.

I feel for people who spend their entire lives measuring their own personal success based on results—results that are being determined by someone else. There's a good chance the criteria being used to measure those results are based on an agenda or on priorities that have nothing whatsoever to do with ability or level of dedication. Let's take two examples. One company may require you to do things that you would never ordinarily do, such as to cut corners, fudge figures, settle for slipshod procedures, or whatever else it takes to jack up a project's numbers or those quarterly earnings. But you do it, and you meet the numbers, and you get the kudos. Now let's take another approach, which involves saying up front that making that number will take longer and cost more, and that there are no prudent short cuts for getting there. Should you be rewarded any less for your honesty, and for advocating a sustainable way to build profits? In such cases, it is often a lack of conscientiousness that's apt to be rewarded, rather than the other way around. And the ultimate results of that can be seen in the corporate scandals that have led to so many firms either falling from grace or being placed under a cloud of suspicion.

Have you ever been in a meeting when the first number of next year's plan wasn't high enough? I have to admit that on many occasions as a CEO I have challenged and rushed, coerced, did whatever it took to get a higher number, only to set everyone up for disappointment. Upon reflection, shame on me for the number of people that I negatively impacted with crazy, short-term schemes just to try to come up with a number investors would like. One vice president who worked for me summed it up best. "Anthony," he said, "you call me about sales—I end up yelling at my wife, and she in turn kicks the dog."

What detaching from results does is enable you to view your working environment from a more objective perspective, better understand the motives (ulterior and otherwise) involved in rewarding or punishing employees, and not take it personally when (a) you can't come up with the "numbers" that are supposedly expected of you, or (b) your best efforts go unappreciated—or perhaps even result in your being admonished. The detachment principle is one that helps you to stay "on mission"—whether it's your personal mission or that of the company your work for.

Remember—the results you achieve when in corporate employ are no more "yours" than is the company itself. In most corporations, your role is merely that of an instrument for achieving certain results, which may not necessarily jibe with either the company's supposed mission or with your own ideas of getting the job done right—and which in any event are subject to both inside and outside pressures and influences that usually have nothing to do with you. And that's OK—it's the way the system is designed. You just have to keep this firmly in mind so you don't start thinking of the company's results as your personal ones. In a sense, no matter how much of a key player you may seem to be, the design of those boxes is to assure the continuity of the system. That may be a good thing in one respect, but by its very nature, it renders you expendable. It's sad but true that in this environment, people are essentially replaceable parts, and shareholders wouldn't have it any other way.

It is important that you understand that this is how things work in a controlling culture, because if you do not have an attitude that is reciprocal, you're setting yourself up for significant disappointment. You simply can't afford to give your heart and soul to a company that has no heart and soul—even one that collectively refers to you and your colleagues as a "family." You have to realize that the company is designed to survive without you, and that you should likewise think in terms of surviving without the company, should that become necessary. And most of all, unless you're the CEO, you have to stop feeling personally responsible for corporate results that have many moving parts.

That doesn't in any way mean you shouldn't take pride in your work and do the best possible job, commit yourself wholeheartedly to the task at hand, or strive to complete it in a manner that offers you satisfaction and is consistent with your true self. It is just to say that you should develop other priorities so that the job does not become your only source of pride or fulfillment or happiness. Ideally, it should only provide you with a part of your daily quota of either commodity. That's because when you work for a group of individuals with different priorities and agenda, there may be times when you become insecure and start to wonder if you are doing the right thing or if you will ever get a pat on the back (which we all need on occasion). This is where the advice offered in Exercise 2 about finding other outlets for achievement and creativity and developing your own inner resources comes into play. Such inner resources are precisely what have always enabled independent achievers, ranging from Thoreau to Colonel Sanders, to give short shrift to short-term considerations in the realization of their individual visions.

In essence, if you want to keep the pursuit of job-related objectives from being hazardous to your physical and mental health, you've got to create a psychological buffer zone that keeps you from becoming too emotionally wrapped up in the results—whether they're negative or positive. To create such a zone, you must first realize that the benchmark separating a positive from a negative result is totally contrived, a mere reflection of somebody asserting their ego. Try to determine whose ego was responsible for setting it. Then you must ask yourself if meeting this standard will in any way have a material impact on your personal mission over the next 10 years—which would be the only reason to become emotionally attached to it. In other words, recognize the motive, and extend the timeline.

You've also got to avoid putting all—or even most—of your own 'ego eggs' in one very precarious corporate basket by not relying on job-related activities solely for personal fulfillment. This will better enable you to avoid becoming frustrated and take it in stride when your pet project is shunted aside, shot down or mangled beyond recognition by company brass (or, in some cases, lawyers).

The silver lining in a corporate picture clouded by corruption

"There is something to be said for the wave of corporate scandals sweeping America … Maybe it will encourage corporate workaholics to do some other things with their lives … Measuring ourselves entirely on the basis of our positions in a company or on our investments is a slender reed to lean on, if you accept the assertion that mortality rates approach 100 percent. Eternal fulfillment is unlikely to come from the stock market or from a series of job promotions … No matter how many loyal employees may trust in them, companies can go poof in a matter of days virtually without warning."
        — *Robert Whitcomb*
        Editorial-page editor, Providence Journal

A personal perspective on the distinction between one's life and one's job

After 12 years as a featured columnist for *The Press of Atlantic City*, Martin DeAngelis was told that the paper had decided to drop his column and reassign him as a reporter. In a farewell column reflecting on his experiences and thanking both his supporters and critics—as well as the editor who had given him both the job and the bad news—DeAngelis noted:

"Sure, I'm disappointed. But to be realistic, a guy getting his job changed registers about a 0.000 on the great Richter scale of human sadness—or way below that. This job was what I did for a living, not who I was in life. That's not a bad thing for all of us to remember sometimes."

The surprising power of the totally objective 'consultant's edge'

There's nothing quite so useful in learning to detach from results as the experience of being a totally objective consultant. Unlike the emotion-laden employee, who is often made to feel that his or her livelihood and validity are tied to performance goals and all too often, office politics, the totally objective consultant has the advantage of being both an independent contractor and observer– and thus a far more objective player in any corporate control drama. It's a feeling that was best expressed during a board meeting I once attended in that capacity, when a board member whom I respected very much turned to me following a comment I had made and said, "Objectivity is a beautiful thing."

Having served large companies as both an employee and a consultant, I'm in a good position to know how much a totally objective consultant's mindset can help a salaried manager or executive to keep a psychological distance between ego and employment. Beyond helping the individual to maintain his or her equilibrium through whatever turbulence the job may involve, however, the stabilizing influence it affords can provide an actual advantage when it comes to winning the "numbers game."

That edge is one that has served me well on a number of occasions. Not too long ago, for example, I served as a consultant in negotiations involving the proposed acquisition of a public company by another firm. I had initially presented a recommendation to a management group, only to have its members huddle up in a defensive posture. Everyone immediately jumped on all the reasons why this was not a good idea, and why the company was not an especially good one to acquire.

My response was to say, "Look, everyone, I have no particular attachment to the outcome of this; it's simply a recommendation, a proposal, and whether you want it or not is strictly up to you. I have no emotional attachment to it." My saying that immediately produced quizzical looks from those present—but it also seemed to liberate them. It was almost as if they had built up a resistance to being "sold" on anything by someone with a personal interest in closing the deal.

But once my objectivity as a consultant had been established, they no longer seemed threatened by my presentation, let down their defenses, and considered the merits of the proposal. In no time flat, the prevailing attitude switched from negative to positive.

An even more dramatic illustration of how persuasive such a detached attitude can be was what happened recently when I was involved in negotiating another such agreement for a client company. As it happened, I was quite convinced that the proposition would be an excellent one for all parties involved—but as an outsider, I could afford to take a cool and dispassionate attitude toward whatever happened. I had been dealing directly with the other party's attorney and after more than three months of negotiations, it all boiled down to one point that could prove to be a deal breaker. For a few days, the situation became rather ugly, since the company that had retained me had spent considerable money on the acquisition involved and was already in the marketing cycle. Now came this major roadblock, with the CEO and CFO of my client company unwilling to give an inch on this one point, and the other firm indicating via e-mail to all involved that without a resolution, the deal was off. It was an extremely disappointing development.

The following day, I got a call from the other party's lawyer, who wanted to know whether there was any point in talking further. I replied, "Well, I have argued this point the best I can. But you have to understand that I am not personally attached to the outcome. It is what it is, and the only thing I can assume right now is that this is the way it was meant to be, and it's not supposed to be a deal. So we'll simply move on and insert something else in its place." As soon as I said that—having concluded a couple days before that I was not going to force the issue, and not even having bothered to call him—his demeanor suddenly changed. He kept his cool, but seemed a little taken aback—in fact, a lot taken aback. "You've got to be kidding me," he said. "After we've been negotiating this for three months, and with all the money your client has already spent?" And then, amazingly enough, he immediately caved in on the point in dispute, and we started discussing putting the deal back together.

Yet another example of how detaching from the outcome offers an amazing leverage in all situations is a recent experience I had in dealing with the CEO of a firm whose management group had hired me as a consultant. The group had taken a position on a particular issue with which I was in total agreement—but the CEO was just as adamant in his opposition to it, which the management group couldn't understand at all. Finally, I decided it would be in everybody's best interest if I were to represent the group by taking the matter up directly with the CEO—and indicate my willingness to terminate my involvement on the spot if that proved necessary. After notifying the company's chief financial officer of my intentions, I proceeded to confront the CEO and let him know where I stood. Again, by virtue of being "unattached," with strong opinions but no personal stake in either the outcome or, for that matter, the company itself, I was able to break through the barrier of resistance—and get a resolution that worked to the benefit of the entire management group.

No doubt about it—detachment from results can be a positive and powerful force. It can save you a lot of time and energy and enable you to negotiate from a position of psychological strength. And, perversely enough, as the above experiences demonstrate, you'll find that when it stops mattering to you how things turn out in your job, you may end up being far more effective than you might ever have anticipated. In short, it's a mindset that's truly liberating, as you'll discover when people ask, "How are you able to smile at a time like this?" or "How do you manage to stay so cool under fire?"

But how does one go about detaching in today's high-stress corporate climate? My recommendation is that you link your personal mission together with the fact that you have to make a living—in a sense, to support it. Then, start regarding your corporate role as being that of someone holding a totally objective perspective, rather than an emotional employee, as reflected in your attitude and the way you deal with situations that arise (always remembering that the numbers weren't divinely ordained, but in most cases merely set by a higher-up). If you're working for a tightly controlled—or controlling—company or individual, there's all the more reason to do so, and to transfer your sense of attachment as an employee to your own personal mission—that is, unless you're fortunate enough to be working for a firm whose mission correlates with yours , in which case a feeling of genuine attachment to your job may be somewhat justified (but only with the awareness that even the most ideal of corporate circumstances are subject to changes beyond your control).

By changing the way you view yourself and your contributions, you'll soon come to the realization that whatever happens in your corporate environment, it's not about you, whereas your personal mission is. Armed with that awareness, you can work to make your living without allowing your work to be what you live for—and have people wondering why you are smiling.

The dot.com disaster: A fast-buck fiasco

Nothing better demonstrates how counter-productive the emphasis on short-term results can be than the bursting of the Internet or dot.com bubble –a bubble that simply couldn't survive the speed or force with which it was being inflated by people with a get-rich-quick philosophy.

I speak from personal experience, as I and a friend, the ex-CEO of a chain of restaurants, were intrinsically involved in that fiasco—put in a position of seeing what we both thought was a viable and original Web service concept get overblown and prematurely launched by venture capitalists intent on making a quick killing.

The endeavor was called TruCost Systems—a proposition that I first conceived on a flight from Charlotte to Los Angeles. It was a way for independent restaurant operators, using zip codes and product specifications, to know what part of their revenue they should be giving their distributors. But the minute the venture capitalists became involved, the race was on to make a fast buck, and the project became all about form, rather than substance—about speed, rather than building something for the future. It became a matter of trying every day and every week to meet impossible milestones, everyone working very hard to reach unattainable short-term goals.

Adding to the disappointment was the way in which the money interests would constantly shift direction. Bill, who ran the day-to-day operation and who gave it the benefit of his experience as one of the best "people managers" in the restaurant business, described it as a case of "ego and greed overshadowing a great fundamental business model" in which he attempted to protect himself and the employees "from the short-term madness and focus on building a business for the next 50 years, not the next five." Once the dust settles, he adds, "that is still what I intend to do."

How detaching from apparent failure can turn it your advantage

Had Colonel Sanders' restaurant business not ended in failure, Kentucky Fried Chicken would in all likelihood have remained a commodity not much known beyond the vicinity of Corbin, Kentucky—and he would have lived the rest of his life in relative obscurity. But then again, many a success story has been built on an apparent failure—or even a series of them. That's why the negative connotation usually attached to someone having "failed" is so often just another example of short-term thinking.

The problem comes in allowing that limited perception of failure to infiltrate your psyche—to make you feel somehow deficient, inadequate or incompetent if you're unable to live up to some contrived standard, goal or expectation established by other people, either arbitrarily or to satisfy some hidden agenda. When that happens, and you go around wearing the albatross of failure around your neck, it can be an inhibiting factor, weighing you down and blocking the flow of psychic and physical energy you need to move on with your life and career.

If, on the other hand, you can psychologically detach from failure, you'll be in a good position to benefit from the experience by viewing it objectively, determining what part of it—or, indeed, if any of it—was a result of your mistakes or misreading of the situation, and learning what pitfalls to avoid. Then failure can actually become one of your building blocks.

Sometimes you may find that what seems to be failure is due to nothing more than a bad ego trip on your part. You may have thought you could handle a situation to everyone's satisfaction when, in fact, an overdose of self-confidence caused you to underestimate the obstacles or misinterpret the scenario or the motives of the other players involved.

Such hubris was undoubtedly a major factor in my " failed" tenure as CEO of The New Organics Company that I poured my heart and soul into for two years. Despite having excellent products and a great group of investors, I was unable to turn its fortunes around. The company, I have since realized, was doomed from its inception by the marketing strategies implemented by its original managers—people with conventional food-industry experience who shunned the distribution methods used by successful producers of natural/organic commodities. By the time I came aboard, the die was already cast—yet I was egotistical enough to think I could somehow fix things. But it really wasn't about me. No matter how good I thought I was, the course had already been set, the iceberg was dead ahead, and I wasn't in a position to do anything but watch the company go down and try to organize the evacuation. (I remember once telling the lead investor that I would stay with the firm until I had to turn the lights off, little knowing how true that would turn out to be.)

Five months after announcing the closing of The New Organics Company, I was faced with whether I could actually "walk the talk." A speaking engagement I had accepted while I was still CEO was looming ahead. To prepare for it, I spent time evaluating the entire period of my stint at the company in order to emotionally detach from the experience—and succeeded to the point where I could objectively recount it before the annual meeting of the Organics Trade Association in Austin, Texas (some of whose members had been put off by a perceived arrogance on the part of New Organics—an attitude that "we know better"). I noted the lessons I had taken away from this particular experience, starting with the original managers' arrogance in their "go-to-market" strategy, then emphasizing my own egotism in thinking I could somehow fix the results. I had come to regard this whole ordeal as a positive rather than a painful experience—and made a promise to myself that I would do everything I could so people could learn from it. And, in fact, it has proved quite valuable to me in my subsequent involvement in the promotion of organic agriculture, which is now deeply imbedded in my personal mission.

If, on the other hand, I had allowed the failure of The New Organics Company to become my own personal failure, I might have decided that I was not suited to participate in the organic industry—and thus exiled myself from further participation in what I believe is the single most significant and meaningful development in modern food production.

Another more recent example is what resulted from the apparent failure of a "white paper" that a group of us had been awarded a grant to produce. It was to have been a precedent-setting report on how the raising of natural beef could benefit rural communities in the U.S., which a group of experts had been assembled to compile. But we were unable to surmount the degree of resistance we encountered from ranchers in rural areas, which was both fascinating and demoralizing. Within this apparently failed white paper, however, was a recommendation for the launching of a pet-food company that would utilize the antibiotic-and-hormone-free meat and chicken we had discussed. This led to the formation of the Natural Pet Nutrition Co, one of the first truly holistic pet food operations in the country.

One more thing on the subject of failure: If you can't shake the feeling that you're somehow remiss for not having met your "numbers" or some other standard of performance set by your superiors—or feel that you must give up your life and your sleep to meet those expectations— just think of the CEOs of companies whose stock has tumbled to a small fraction of its former value under their stewardship, or which have been caught engaging in creative accounting practices that have brought them to ruin. If they have no embarrassment or compunctions about being richly rewarded for the highly visible failures of their companies—about continuing to collect large salaries, leaving with multi-million dollar golden parachutes and in either event living the high life while their shareholders and employees see their livelihoods, savings and retirement funds go up in smoke—why should you feel put down, chagrined or self-conscious when you've done your best, and your best just wasn't good enough?

But just as you shouldn't take such seeming failures to heart, nei- ther should you allow it to go to your head when you're exceeding your numbers, realizing far better results than you had anticipated or get- ting a promotion. Keep in mind that succeeding, too, can sometimes prove to be an illusion—especially in an economy where the rug can suddenly be pulled out from under the most impressive entities. Remember, in the corporate culture, failure and success are opposite sides of the same coin, which is apt to be flipped by the people at the helm. You're best off emotionally detaching from either type of out- come—and finding true fulfillment in aspects of living other than what you do for a living.

Detachment from results allows you to be objective and to view all aspects of your job and the culture surrounding it from the proper perspective Having this perspective will allow you to focus on what matters most— your personal mission and striving toward your vision. You are no longer going to be judging success or failure by someone else's yard- stick—or letting someone else's goals or quarterly numbers impact your attitude, health or life.

Now you're ready to know more (people, that is)

Without an emotional attachment to either your company or the results you achieve at work, you'll find control and fear dissolving before your eyes. You have reaffirmed your mission, are moving toward your vision, taking time to be healthy and creative, and have cultivated a positive new attitude as a result. Having thus empowered yourself, you are now ready to expand the reach and scope of something that counts for a lot—your network of friends and acquaintances.

Who said failure is not an option?

To emotionally detach from a seemingly failed effort in your job, all you need is the realization of just how universal such failure is. It's something I discovered for myself at a convention when I decided to give a talk on all the product failures in which I had been involved. Wow, what a strange feeling to publicly describe each one! The interesting thing is that I got into the rhythm of recounting all my mistakes. I started to have fun with the audience at my own expense. Several months later, I was told that it was the highest rated talk at the convention. Two years later, an individual whom I had just met said, "I know you. You're the guy with all the product failures." And to think you feel chagrined just because you're part of a division that failed to meet its numbers!

"Success has many fathers, but failure is an orphan"
— *Anonymous*

In 1985, I led a multidivisional team for a large conglomerate that was developing a new product. We were by far the market leader, but a competitor who five years before was not considered relevant was starting to take share. This company would not sell to us, so we needed a comprehensive plan to displace them in the market. Because the multidivisional group involved was such a great team, the product that was launched is today an incredibly successful brand garnering itself a $250 million share of a billion-dollar category. Although nearly two decades have passed since the product first appeared, I cannot tell you how many people I have met who talk about their role in this project or share the credit for it on their resumes. Most, however, did not know one single person on the original team that conceived the product and brought it to market. As a result, it would be difficult for anyone who was actually instrumental in this accomplishment to claim the credit they rightfully deserve—providing another illustration of what a mistake it is to become too emotionally attached to anything that happens on the job, be it success or failure (especially when your role is part of a group effort, as is usually the case).

Some tips on detaching from the numbers game

1. Avoid letting the issue of whether you or your company is meeting its "numbers" affect your morale or sense of well-being.

2. Remember: You are not a number, and meeting the numbers is not about you. When you let the numbers attach themselves to you, you can't be objective.

3. When someone tries to tell you that you have to meet a certain number, think through to the source. Ask yourself what the agenda is, and to whom it is so important.

4. Regard yourself as being an employee of your own personal mission statement. The attitude of objectivity and distance will help you to smile, even in tight situations.

5. Remember, there is a seed of success in every failure. Make sure you are emotionally detached enough to cultivate that seed.

Reflections: Exercise 4

Make a list of successes at your job in the last year or so. Then make a list of successes outside of work.

Successful Results at Work	Successes Outside of Work
_____	_____
_____	_____
_____	_____
_____	_____
_____	_____
_____	_____
_____	_____
_____	_____

If success at work outweighs success outside of work, reminding yourself of your personal mission is imperative.

Think about your last so-called 'failure' at your job. How did you respond to it? How might you have responded to it?

_____

_____

_____

_____

_____

Did you learn anything from the above failure? What might you have learned?

_____

_____

_____

_____

_____

_____

_____

_____

_____

_____

_____

_____

_____

_____

Exercise 5

Develop Your 'People Options'

Alleviating your fear of being fired by having a collection of connections

Summary

1. Recognize how important a personal network of friends, acquaintances and business contacts can be to anything you want to accomplish.

2. Make a point of building your own network of "people options" grounded in such old-fashioned values as mutual trust, honesty, shared interests or recollections, friendship, and genuine regard, rather than mere mercenary interaction. Help others to build their networks as well.

3. Add to your 'collection of connections' by actively cultivating relationships with as broad a range of people as possible—and by paying attention to those you encounter in different situations who could turn out to have a significant influence on your life.

4. Make a point of maintaining your network on a quarterly basis via e-mail—as well as by calling and meeting with people every so often and by sending out cards on holidays and other occasions.

5. Don't allow yourself to be put off by negative first impressions.

6. Remember that an ounce of civility toward adversaries can be worth a ton of combat strategy.

7. Treat everyone you meet with respect, realizing that leaders and potentially valuable allies can be found in the seemingly unlikeliest of circumstances—and sometimes by simply going out of your way for people.

"We may all have come on different ships, but we're in the same boat now."
— Dr. Martin Luther King Jr.

One of the most upbeat and liberating aspects of serving a corporation while trying to keep it from taking over your life is that there are millions of other people, at all different stages in life, who are going through similar experiences. And as in any large-scale mutual survival effort, they want to help you and hope that you can do likewise for them. Either one, however, requires that you wake up, heed the signals they're sending you, and reach out to them. Perhaps the person who will play a crucial role in your future—or your mission—just left you a phone message or sat down next to you at lunch. It is an innate, natural instinct for all of us to want to help each other. Sometimes, we just have to crack through the exterior. One of the best techniques for doing that is networking with the ultimate purpose of creating a mechanism for mutual assistance. Making such an effort seems to give people a new appreciation of you—and by helping others in this way, you also help yourself.

As noted in Exercise 3, this network of contacts is the most important tool you have to help you to overcome the fear of being fired—one of the key control mechanisms that unconsciously characterizes all corporations. The more people with whom you network, the greater your opportunities to find both a position that's more consistent with your mission, and to surround yourself with the kind of honest, professional and non-manipulative associates with whom you can more readily identify (and whose company you genuinely enjoy). You never know when having a little help from your friends may make the crucial difference in getting by—or succeeding in your mission.

That's why it's so important to devote a certain amount of time every week to building your Rolodex. Once you've firmly established your mission and vision, begun the process of getting yourself in better shape and learned how to take evasive action against corporate-control attempts, the collection of connections it contains may well prove to be your most valuable asset.

From 'catchy' title to successful chain—via a crucial link to my past

While movies have often been known to result in transitory fads, the film "Forrest Gump" had a much more lasting effect. It was the inspiration for the highly successful Bubba-Gump Shrimp Restaurant chain—the subject of considerable media attention, including a *Time* magazine "Trend of the Year" article and a *New York Times* cover story, "Art Comes to Life." But if the Bubba-Gump phenomenon was an example of life imitating art, it was also an illustration of the key role that networking—the art of cultivating and maintaining your own personal garden of connections—can play in the favorable outcome of a venture. I know first-hand, because I had the great fortune to be intrinsically involved in the saga.

It began when I put together a licensing agreement for use of the name between Paramount and Meridian Products, a large importer and exporter of frozen shrimp. Within six weeks of getting the license, Meridian was selling frozen Bubba Gump shrimp everywhere in the country. The shrimp were sold in conjunction with tee-shirts and hats from Tuff Shirt, whose owner, Kenny Lee, and I became close friends. Kenny and I enjoyed the ride on a tidal wave of movie-generated publicity and exposure. But those of us who were involved—including Paramount Pictures—saw an opportunity to expand the phenomenon's potential beyond that of a mere quick trend or fad.

It wasn't an original idea, but rather one that came when I was approached by a fast-seafood chain that was interested in using the name. We all agreed that a restaurant named "Bubba Gump Shrimp Co." could outlive the movie-generated hype. After weeks of debating the proposition, however, Paramount decided that the seafood chain that had approached us wasn't quite the type of operation they had in mind for the image of Bubba Gump. But if one restaurant chain was interested, we were certain other restaurateurs would be—and that Kenny and I would eventually find the one that meshed with our ideas while maintaining the economic viability of our interest in the enterprise.

Working with Paramount to construct a list of potential friendly partners, several of us got busy calling various people we knew in the restaurant industry. Most of the direct contacts I made said no to the proposition. But one former associate of mine, Gordon Miles, then chairman of the Rusty Pelican Restaurants and former chairman of the Paragon Restaurant Group, did become interested. Gordon and I had worked together from 1986 through 1990, when I was president of Pacific Basin Foods, the company that managed the food-product and supply chain for his restaurants. It was a long enough time for me to appreciate how resourceful he could be and the unique enthusiasm he could bring to the enterprise. But first, he had to sell the president and management team of the Rusty Pelican on the idea's merits. They were entrenched in the Rusty Pelican mind-set and had trouble seeing the concept that both Gordon and I envisioned. Helping to bring them on board was my first assignment.

The second was much more difficult—persuading Paramount that Gordon and the Rusty Pelican were the right partner, despite having just emerged from bankruptcy. We rehearsed the presentation many times and finally succeeded in getting the Rusty Pelican the license.

When the opening party for the very first Bubba Gump Shrimp Company restaurant took place in Monterey, very few of those who attended were aware of all the behind-the-scene dynamics. As limos pulled up carrying Paramount's top brass—Chairman Sherry Lansing and Viacom Entertainment Group Chairman Johnathan Dolgen—Gordon had the glow of a man who had accomplished a major feat. And in my mind I knew that even with all the Hollywood hoopla, it would never have happened without Gordon and me working behind the scenes. The chain has since become extremely successful, with its 11 sites grossing some of the highest weekly sales of any restaurants in the business. But it might not have worked out that way had not Gordon and I continued to stay in touch after our original professional affiliation had ended.

The success of the chain served as an important calling card for me. Our having recruited the right partner for the real-life version of Bubba Gump Shrimp Co. proved what can be achieved by continuously building and maintaining an active network of "people options"—whether they be close friends, casual acquaintances or business contacts. In fact, I consider such a collection of connections to be the most valuable asset you can possibly have when it comes to stabilizing and advancing your career, fulfilling your mission and generally enjoying your life. **So allow me to emphasize this again:** *Your collection of associates, friends, and acquaintances can be the most important asset you can possibly have.*

By a network, I'm not referring to the kind of contacts whose loyalties can be bought and sold like major-league ballplayers. I have seen examples of that, such as one company I was hired to turn around and take out of bankruptcy, only to learn that its principals had failed to build up any sort of reservoir of good will and had to rely strictly on paying people off. Nor is it enough to simply know different people in your particular area of endeavor like Ebenezer Scrooge, whose contacts were limited to perfunctory associations with other businessmen prior to his ghostly visitations. The connections I'm referring to are those that work through such old-fashioned values as mutual trust, honesty, sincerity, shared interests or recollections, friendship and genuine regard—the kinds of relationships that are their own reward but can, and often do lead to material ones as well. When you are working with a group that shares such intrinsic attributes, you can speak in a kind of shorthand that eliminates so many perfunctory steps and all that 'busy work' that's ordinarily involved in having to deal with people. The ability to engage in this type of relating is truly a blessing, and one you can enjoy for its own sake.

Your network will also provide you with your own personal support group—a resource that can act as a sort of counterweight to the oppressive influence of corporate control, and make it easier for you to get through tough times or difficult situations. Because the bigger your network of people options, the more likely you are to know individuals who have "been there"—and who can offer you assistance, advice or moral support in handling certain types of control scenarios. That's especially true when the screws get tightened, and the circle of people you're dealing with gets smaller and smaller, in which case you need to involve more people in the process, working from the sidelines as advisers and advocates.

Missed connections may be missed opportunities

Your most likely shot at landing the kind of opportunity you are looking for, assuming you have all the requisite qualifications, is to know somebody who can provide you with the proper insight or angle for snaring it. While it may not be absolutely true that "you gotta have connections" to get into the movie business, or, quite frankly, any business, it certainly does help to know the right people. That's true, in fact, of any elite area of endeavor. But, without having the advantage of being born into a cinematic or theatrical family, how does one go about making such connections in the first place?

The best way, as it turns out, may be by building one's peer group so that it includes as broad and diverse a range of people as possible, some of whom may either go on to become prime movers and shakers—captains of industry, influential politicians or government officials, or perhaps even big names in show biz—or who might be in a position to introduce you to such individuals. I was once told that you are only three people away from the very person you need to meet. I believe this and have lived by it ever since. Whenever someone asks me if I know someone, my immediate response if I don't know them is, "No, but I know someone who does"—and invariably, I do.

It really has nothing to do with the celebrity factor, but may be as simple as sitting next to the right person at a seminar, or on a plane, or at a sporting event. This recently happened to my wife Lisa. She had made a decision to follow a life dream and go into acting, but was unable to get an agent's attention—that is, until she attended a seminar on hypnosis. There, she found herself sitting next to an aspiring actor named Cathy Kay, with whom she struck up a conversation. Within three weeks, using Cathy's connections, Lisa had gotten an agent—and was off doing auditions.

As it turns out, we all have the opportunity to form such relationships. I find it quite interesting how often we are touched in some way by ordinary people doing extraordinary things. If we pay attention, we will realize that we are constantly surrounded by individuals who can either assist us in carrying out our own personal missions or who know others that can do so. I love being reminded of this fact, as when I chanced to exchange Web sites with one of my kickboxing partners. When I got home, I looked his up. He turned out to be author Phil Reed, whose books included "Free Throw," the story about the 72-year-old who set a world record by sinking 2,750 shots in a row.

This phenomenon gave me chills while viewing a movie called *Almost Famous* at a theater a couple of years ago. As I watched, I was struck by a feeling of intense familiarity with the setting. Not only had the scenes been shot in Ocean Beach, a part of San Diego where I grew up, but the high school shown was the one I had attended. Beyond being mesmerized, I was convinced that someone I once knew had to be involved in making this picture. I immediately went home and took out my high-school yearbook, and sure enough, there was Cameron Crow—a photographer and writer for the school newspaper I had known as a classmate, but with whom I had formed no personal relationship. Now, here he was, not only the writer and director of the film I had just seen, but the celebrated director of Tom Cruise in *Jerry Maguire* and the soon-to-be-released *Vanilla Sky*.

Nor was that the only time I was reminded that people you meet every day may be extraordinary. A number of years ago (wow—27 at the time of this writing, to be precise) I became casually acquainted with a young woman named Kathleen, who was a friend of a girlfriend of mine. I had heard she was very driven—she had a lot she wanted to do, and was determined to do it. She had just left her job at a local news station in San Diego and there was a going-away party for her, which I happened to attend. I didn't know her that well, but when we sat down on the couch at the house where the party was taking place, she started telling me some things I found quite intriguing. She was planning on moving to Los Angeles, even though she had no job prospects there and didn't know specifically what she was going to be doing. All she did know was that whatever the future held in store for her, it was going to be bigger and better and more important than what she was doing in San Diego. You might even say she was on a mission, although she hadn't quite got around to defining what it was. I do recall that I admired the gumption and ambition she exhibited—but never really bothered to follow up on the conversation we had that night.

Well, she did move to L.A., and ended up working for a guy named Steven Spielberg. And when his classic film *E.T.* came out a few years later, the producer was none other than Kathleen—Kathleen Kennedy. She has since gone on to head a successful production company that has been responsible for a number of films, such as *The Sixth Sense*. Having been so impressed by her attitude when we chatted that evening, I was delighted to learn of her subsequent success in the movie industry.

I cite these examples only to illustrate my point: Every day, you are apt to come into contact with someone who might profoundly influence your life in some way, if only indirectly. For instance, that individual could introduce you to somebody who might, in turn, get you together with someone else who is in a position to help you—or your mission. Those hollow eyes you encounter in the mall, on an airplane or standing in line could end up opening yours to new horizons. But you'll never know if all you do is exchange greetings, or pleasantries, and move on.

One of my biggest regrets, in fact, is that I didn't get around to making networking part of my work routine until I was almost 38 years old. The potential connections I missed out on as a result of this lack of discipline weren't just limited to my not getting to know Cameron Crowe—or following up on my encounter with Kathleen Kennedy. There were, for example, the overlooked opportunities for meeting people in my early thirties during the marketing and business classes that I attended at Northwestern University. The instructors included Al Rappaport, a professor whose claim to fame was evaluating acquisitions on the basis of cash flow—the big buzz word during this particular period. These classes, which weren't exactly cheap, attracted managerial types from all over the country, including senior executives and other people on the fast track at firms like UPS and W.R. Grace, as well as all the major conglomerates. Not being tuned in at the time to how valuable such personal contacts could be, however, I spent my time focusing on what I was there to learn and meeting with my study group at night. I had neither the time nor inclination to socialize at the cocktail party, for instance, and to make a point of getting to know some of these people, or to position myself for a follow-up. This is so interesting now to look back on. While I was so intent on the curriculum, the most important part of this executive program, I now realize, was the opportunity it offered for networking with key individuals. Had I been "on mission" at the time, just one contact would have been the true benefit I would have gained from the experience, rather than simply learning to understand discounted cash flow.

Once I realized how I had limited myself by failing to take advantage of such opportunities, I began to do everything I could to make up for lost time. I started paying a lot more attention to people, and making a conscious effort to build and expand my personal and professional alliances. Today, my Rolodex contains more than 4,000 names and addresses of people of all ages and in all walks of life—contacts that have been directly responsible for most of the consulting projects that I have taken on. And one of my primary goals has been to maintain my relationships with as many of those individuals as I possibly can, even if just to notify them of a cell-phone number change or my role in an acquisition.

The point is that no matter how reserved or unassertive you've been when it comes to forming associations, it's never too late to become more outgoing, to start connecting, and to broaden your circle of contacts. That doesn't just mean the people with whom you may have had some professional or personal association at one time or another (although it's certainly important to include as many of them as possible in your network), but the contacts you might have occasion to meet through them as well. It can also mean initiating relationships with "perfect strangers" with whom you might discover some common bond (perhaps nothing more substantial than a hobby, an athletic pursuit or some shared literary interest). When you're sitting in an airplane or seminar, for instance, do you keep to yourself or try to get to know the person sitting next to you? Quite possibly, this individual could play some key role in your future, perhaps help you to fulfill a mission or reach an objective—but you'll never know if your tendency is to tune out the people options that might surround you.

Networking tips:

1. *Recalling someone's name always helps to create a favorable impression. When introduced to someone for the first time, a good way of committing their name to memory is to look for one distinguishing characteristic that you can associate with that name.*

2. *Summarize weekly the new people that you have met or old acquaintances with whom you've re-established contact. Make a list, update e-mail and phone numbers weekly, and use follow-up notes.*

How an 'imposition' led to an important connection

Sometimes, the best kinds of connections might be the ones you'll make by going a little bit out of your way for people.

A good example is the time that I was in the middle of a crisis of sorts involving an upcoming vote by an agricultural alliance on whether to support our Family Farm project. Being an intrinsic part of my personal mission, it was a cause to which I did have an emotional attachment, and I was apprehensive about the outcome of the meeting. So when my cell phone rang as I was heading north on Interstate 5 twenty minutes out of Los Angeles, with the caller wanting to know if I would be willing to turn around and pick up one of the attendees at the airport, I was more than a bit annoyed. The last thing I wanted to do right then was spend another hour in the car. But not wishing to appear to be unaccommodating, I turned around and headed toward LAX.

As it turned out, however, my 'pick-up' proved to be quite an affable companion, and we ended up making some great conversation. And since that day, we've not only continued to relate, but have worked on various projects together and have become partners in a holistic pet-food business. In addition, he was on a board that was very influential in some key areas of my work.

The meeting itself was a disaster, just as I had feared—what with multiple agendas, grandstanding, and dissension. At one point, I couldn't take it any more and got up to leave. But the one valuable thing that did come out of it was that out-of-my-way run to the airport and the ongoing personal and professional relationship that resulted with a guy I trust and with whom I can communicate in "trust shorthand."

Your web of contacts: a shield against the threat of termination

Fear of being fired is the chief form of intimidation that emanates from a corporate structure and is used to keep employees under its control. It's always there—that underlying threat of being given a stamp of rejection, and being stripped of both the artificial status and economic support that goes with one's position. I am not sure that—apart from being independently wealthy—there will ever be any way to solve this. But it sure helps to know as many people as you can. The larger your network of professional contacts, the greater your defense against the threat of termination. The more people you know, the more empowered you are, the more options you'll have, the more opportunities you'll become aware of, and the more help and moral support you're apt to receive. In a sense, having a lot of allies in your camp can do the same thing for you that it does for a country—that is, make you less likely to be attacked. I remember being in a meeting with a CEO who said of one individual, "I can't fire him; he knows too many people."

From a personal perspective, I recall a time early in my career when I was blessed with the opportunity to fly first class, and found myself seated next to an accomplished and successful businessman with his own company in Boston. After spending several hours conversing, we parted on the note that if I ever needed a job, I should call him. I followed up that conversation with calls on several occasions, and found the offer still held. And even though I never actually went to work for him, just knowing it was there helped get me through some tight situations by alleviating my fear of being fired.

Later on, went I went to work as a consultant, my collection of connections proved invaluable. I can't tell you how many times I have been retained by companies mostly on the basis of the resources contained in my Roladex.

Don't be so quick to judge—someone special could be behind the mask

Some people, of course, are easier to get to know, while others may put you off by seeming to be aloof. Often, however, that's simply a defense mechanism, and if you judge someone based on it, you might be missing out on a meaningful relationship that can always develop—in fact, most likely, you will.

An acquaintance of mine, for example, whom I'll call Mike, recalled the first impression he had of the guy who hired him at a particular organization, and who was to be his immediate superior—gruff, unfriendly and even a bit ill-tempered. That was the way it was for the first few weeks, at least. But as time went on and Mike refused to let the

man's dour demeanor rattle him, the boss began to show an entirely different side to his personality—one that was a lot more amiable and
accessible than other managerial types in the organization (perhaps
because Mike's boss had also begun to perceive him differently). One
occasion that marked this turning point was when Mike was called in to
the boss's office for what he thought would be a dressing down. Some
employees, it seemed, thought Mike was "nit-picking" in the way he carried out the quality-control responsibilities he had been assigned, and
had complained to the boss about it. The response, however, was not at
all what Mike expected. "Go right on nit-picking," he was told. "I just
wanted to let you know."

Having successfully bridged the gap between coldness and cordiality,
they both kept in touch long after working together. This ultimately led
to recommendations and introductions that proved genuinely useful to
Mike in his career.

Remember, first impressions, like prejudices, can often result in our
forming erroneous perceptions about people. Keep in mind that
someone whom you might be inclined to dismiss as unreceptive,
unapproachable or inconsequential could turn out to be a valued friend
or contact—just as might the person who arouses your admiration during
an initial encounter. In either case, you'll never know if you've started the
ball in motion unless you take the trouble to "follow through."

Cyberspace—a gift from the gods of networking

The art of the "follow through" that is so crucial to forging your network of relationships lends itself to various techniques. But perhaps none
is quite as effective for cultivating and maintaining relationships as that
made possible by today's information technology. I'm talking, of course,
about e-mail.

What e-mail has done is to free personal communication from the
slow, tedious and cumbersome process associated with conventional or
"snail mail" and the intrusiveness (and oftentimes awkwardness) of the
phone call. It allows us the option of breezy, one-line greetings, short
no-nonsense notes, or the opportunity to put our best rhetorical foot
forward—and convey it to the intended recipient effortlessly and
instantaneously, sometimes eliciting an immediate reply. As such, it's a
wonderful tool for keeping people aware of your existence without
encroaching on their time or privacy—and swapping sentiments, anecdotes, bits of news, gossip or information and updates, both of a personal and professional nature. It also has the advantage of enabling you
to forward all manner of articles, documents and dispatches with the

same ease and timeliness—and, when appropriate, to convey them to everyone in your address book at the touch of a button. In fact, I can think of many instances when communications with people might have lapsed entirely, had it not been for the miracle of e-mail (more than compensating for the inconvenience of having to delete all the junk mail "spam" it has spawned).

E-mailing tip:

Make your message a "keeper"—by offering something that the recipient will find interesting, intriguing or just plain helpful.

The manner in which computer technology has enhanced our ability to locate long-lost friends and relatives is yet another of the ways it has helped broaden our range of contacts. Often, that can be done simply by entering the person's name and state in a "search" function—although there are other means for doing so as well, such as a "Classmates" Web site that offers an e-mail link to former high-school and college chums with whom you might wish to get back in touch. Networking with individuals you knew in a "former life," in fact, can occasionally lead to profitable business relationships as well as highly satisfying personal ones.

That's not to say that more traditional methods of networking aren't important as well. These include strategic phone calls—perhaps in response to some particular news concerning an individual (or else affecting them in some way), either good or bad. Phoning and possibly meeting people you know in other parts of the country (or the world) for breakfast, lunch or dinner while you are passing through their particular locale is also an excellent way of strengthening your broad-based network of contacts and connections (and one that I have found particularly helpful in this regard).

Networking tip:

A lost cell phone is a good excuse to e-mail the people on your contact list with a short note containing your new cell-phone number.

Taking the trouble to mail out tasteful holiday cards (or, when indicated, condolence or get-well cards)—especially with personal notes included—is also a highly effective, and often much appreciated way, of keeping in touch. In an age when such traditions seem to be declining, you'll find that the little bit of extra time and effort it takes has a way of impressing people with your thoughtfulness.

Rules for building your Rolodex

Rule 1
The "You, You, You Rule" (a gift to me from Sol Zatt in 1997)
When sending a letter, always make sure the first three sentences are about the party you are writing to before references to "I" come up.

Rule 2
The "At-Your-Service Rule" (a gift from Steve Horowitz in 1995)
Ingratiate yourself with your network contacts by asking the question "What can I do for you" in the course of every call you make.

Rule 3
The Weekly Review Rule
Set aside a time each week to evaluate and list any new contacts you have made during the course of the previous seven days. If possible, follow each one up with an e-mail note.

Rule 4
The 'Name Association' Rule
Whenever you're introduced to someone, make a mental note of some distinguishing characteristic that you can associate with the person's name.

Remember, however, that networking is a two-way street—and it's just as important to be responsive to other people's overtures, even when you're pressed for time or distracted by responsibilities.

An ounce of civility is worth a ton of combat strategy

Anyone whose life is free of conflict or disagreements is probably living a totally isolated existence. And business, by its very nature, is bound to involve situations in which the parties are at odds with each other—be they on the same or opposite sides. But, no matter what's at stake, disputes don't have to be carried on in a discourteous manner. A little civility, in fact, can sometimes provide the key to resolving situations that have reached an impasse by restoring the human connection between adversaries.

It's entirely possible, for instance, that a single act of courtesy and compassion—one that transcended the hostilities of warfare—might have tipped the balance in favor of America's winning its independence from Britain. According to an account provided by Canadian psychology professor Stanley Coren in his book *The Pawprints of History*, it occurred when the Continental Army was about at its lowest point, having lost several key battles and in the process of losing yet another one at Germantown, on the outskirts of Philadelphia. At about this time, a small fox terrier that had strayed into an area between the British and American lines was taken into custody by a colonial soldier, who noticed a tag identifying its owner as none other than British General William Howe, the leader of the opposing forces. The soldier proceeded to take the little dog to General Washington, apparently with the idea that having "captured" the British commander's dog and keeping it as a mascot might improve morale.

Washington, however—himself a dog lover—would have none of it. Instead, he cleaned, brushed and fed the animal, then, ordering a cease-fire, had one of his officers return the dog under a flag of truce with a note that read: "General Washington's compliments to General Howe. General Washington does himself the pleasure to return to him a dog, which accidentally fell into his hands, and, by the inscription on the collar, appears to belong to General Howe." According to one of Howe's aides, there also appeared to have been a second note tucked under the dog's collar whose contents were never revealed, but which seemed to go over quite well with the British commander—as did the return of the dog itself, which Howe would later refer to as "the honorable act of a gentleman."

This incident, Coren noted, resulted in a noticeable change in Howe's attitude toward Washington, and from that day on, he seemed reluctant to pursue the campaign against the revolutionaries nearly as aggressively or press his advantage over his opponent. Eventually, given a direct order to "show such little compassion to the rebels that they will be afraid to do ought but return to the crown," Howe resigned, to be replaced by commanders who weren't nearly as proficient in tactics and who would ultimately lose the war.[6]

The above example is but one illustration of how an ounce of civility can be worth a ton of combat strategy. Conciliatory behavior doesn't have to involve surrender of one's terms or principles, but might just consist of some small concession or even an act of courtesy such as Washington exhibited. At the very least, it can serve to let down your adversary's guard and leave room for the kind of one-on-one negotiating that lawyers tend to discourage, because it can sometimes lead to disputes being resolved without their help.

Remember that someone we regard as an enemy may merely reflect a side of ourselves that we don't like—and are in denial about. That's why we might say they bring out the "worst" in us. If, on the other hand, they bring out our best tendencies, it means we've been courageous enough to manage—and purge—that undesirable aspect of our being.

Keep in mind, too, that business is not a win-lose situation—it never has been, and never will be. And, above all, remember that an adversary may one day turn out to be an ally—as history has so often proven. And when that happens, it's nice to have an ally who thinks of you as "honorable"—and who you can add to your network of people options.

The benefits of becoming a 'matchmaker'

In the process of building your collection of connections, one of the most effective things you can do is to bring people together by networking for others.

Successful people are always serving as 'matchmakers.' Anytime someone contacts you with a question that you can't answer directly, refer them to another party you think might be able to. Whether they can or can't, you will gain a reputation as the person to contact when there's a problem—the one who will get the caller in touch with someone else who might have the solution.

By the same token, you should use social occasions to introduce as many people as possible to others. Such networking for others can't help but put you in high esteem as the person who has the connections—and is willing to share them. By networking for others in this fashion, you end up networking for yourself.

"Don't worry about knowing people; just make yourself worth knowing."
— *Anonymous*

All people matter—and you never know which ones might matter most

It's easy to dismiss people as being unimportant to you, based on their outward appearance, position or condition when you encounter them. In so doing, however, you not only might be throwing away a valuable contact, but tempting fate to make you look like an utter fool as well. The late Supreme Court Justice William O. Douglas, for instance, recounted how disconcerting it was for a small-town doctor to discover Douglas' identity, having assumed he was a bum when the justice came in to have a blister on his foot treated after his car had broken down en route to a camping expedition.[7]

Conversely, you never know what might result from the act of extending a hand to someone—even many years later. An example is the assistance that was given to a young man named Schmuel Gelbfisz, who arrived penniless in Hamburg, Germany, after having walked about 500 miles from his hometown of Warsaw, Poland, determined to somehow realize his dream of getting to America—a dream harbored by countless other impoverished people from Eastern Europe in 1895. Wandering the streets of the German port, he finally found a shop bearing the name given to him by his mother before leaving home—that of a former Warsaw family who had migrated there earlier. Entering "with my ragged clothes and dirty, tear-stained face," as he later put it, he told the proprietor, "I am on my way to America and I won't go back." Responding to the young wayfarer's plea for assistance, Jacob Liebglid, the shop's owner, offered him refuge and spent the next few weeks showing him the basics of his trade, glovemaking. When it became apparent, however, that the lad was intent on moving on, Liebglid, himself in no financial position to help, went a step further, canvassing the neighborhood to raise the 18 shillings the boy needed to board a boat train to London.

A half century later, the two would meet again—in a fading luxury hotel in the upstate New York city of Gloversville, where Libglid (who had dropped the 'e' from his name) was living, still plying his trade. The man he had once helped make it to America (before eventually taking the same route himself) was in town for a trip down memory lane, to meet a former employer in the glovemaking industry for dinner and to give a speech to a local men's club, when he was told there was someone there who wanted to know if he remembered Hamburg. A month after the reunion that followed, Libglid received from Tiffany's a $200 gold pocket watch—one he subsequently showed to everyone he met—inscribed with his name and the words "A FRIEND INDEED. SAMUEL GOLDWYN." And as his former benefactor's health declined, the fabled movie mogul would continue to send him money regularly until his death a few years later.[8]

What these anecdotes underscore is the importance of treating everyone you meet with respect, realizing that leaders and potentially valuable allies can be found in the seemingly unlikeliest of circumstances and scenarios. That's not to say that everyone you encounter is apt to be a present or future Supreme Court justice or Hollywood producer. But it is to make the observation that all people matter—and that some of those you casually come in contact with may matter a great deal more than is evident from their situation or their appearance. Hence my recommendation: Do not cavalierly dismiss anyone you come in contact with—and never underestimate how important the little things you do can be to other people (and, ultimately, to you as well).

In addition, helping to enable someone else's spirit is a liberating experience—it just plain feels good. It's a reminder that all of us are connected—and that the connections we have with each other are far more substantial and meaningful than the artifices that we use as barriers, which are usually attached to us by the corporations for which we work.

I happen to be a big fan of Muhammad Ali—and the reason became quite apparent to me when I recently watched the movie made about his career. The thing about him is that he related to everybody—he really talked to people and looked them right in the eye as he did so. He may have been screaming or blurting something out, but he was talking directly to you. In fact, he went out of his way—or seemed to, in any event—to make eye contact with onlookers during his workouts. And I found it quite interesting that he was portrayed that way in the movie—when there were guards lined up as he walked out, for instance, he was depicted as going up to each of them, shaking their hand and saying hello. Perhaps that's what made him such an icon.

That ability to connect with people is a little bit like a nuclear chain reaction, in that it tends to bring all the people in the vicinity out of themselves. And you don't have to be a world champion to do it. I know of a young lady who works in a coffee shop that I frequent (in fact, I do a lot of my writing and strategic analysis at this particular coffee shop). Not only is she a hard and conscientious worker, but she knows most of the customers by name—and usually something personal about them as well. And she manages to make the simple experience of going in there for breakfast or a cup of coffee something special. This girl is probably in her early twenties, and the impact she has on everybody is absolutely amazing.

So when you're building your network of people options, be sure and leave some room for the "coffee shop connection." Who knows—with that kind of charisma and ability to make people feel good about themselves, she just might turn out to be tomorrow's Kathleen Kennedy—or perhaps even your next boss.

The merging of two missions: a networking nexus

When Robert Gulay brought his two-year-old son into a Trenton, N.J. emergency room with a raging fever and terrible congestion one night some years ago, little did he suspect how profound the repercussions would be from that visit—nor did Dr. William Toreki, the attending physician at the time.

But as a result of Dr. Toreki's success in treating the child's life-threatening bronchial infection, and thus becoming the family's pediatrician, the separate missions of both men would merge in a way that would help save the lives of people living half a world away.

In 1993, Toreki, having taken an administrative position at New Jersey's Southern Ocean County Hospital, observed something he found highly disturbing—a number of perfectly sound heart monitoring machines, which had been replaced with state-of-the-art equipment, sitting in a hallway waiting to be disposed of. He felt the equipment could be put to use where it was desperately needed—in the ill-supplied hospitals of the former Soviet Union. "I went down a list of people that I knew," he later recalled. And when he got to Gulay, the latter "seemed very excited. He literally bubbled with enthusiasm."

That was because Gulay, as trustee chairman of the New Jersey Ukrainian American Veterans, had already taken part in the delivery of medical supplies to the Ukraine through an organization called "Children of Chernobyl"—and his post had at that very moment begun making inquiries regarding the availability of just such surplus hospital equipment.

Gulay, in turn, proceeded to call one of his contacts in the Washington, D.C. area, and through him, was connected to a Ukrainian woman pediatrician who was in the U.S. taking her certification exams—and who managed to get a commitment from the chief doctor of her hospital back home, the Zaporizhia Children's Hospital. With that in place, Gulay's UAV post was instrumental in arranging for a military transport to ship the delicate machines to the Ukraine, where technicians had them rewired and up and running in a matter of days.

But the effort didn't end there. In the months and years that followed, millions of dollars worth of donated medical equipment and supplies arrived in Zaporizhia. It was, in fact, the beginning of the New Jersey Adopt-a-Hospital program, whose mission was to improve the quality of health care for the people of the former Soviet Union, and particularly the victims of the Chernobyl disaster.

And all made possible through the power of networking.

Now go on and amuse yourself

Let's review how far you've come. You've determined your mission and vision, and embarked on a campaign to turn them both into reality. You've also come to realize that your job is not really you, and taken certain steps to mentally and emotionally detach yourself from corporate control and the ways success and failure are measured in your work. And you've gone about cultivating the collection of connections that can help you to survive, accomplish your mission and perhaps provide you with other options should you be forced to part company with the company for which you now work.

Now why don't you take a break. You sound as if you could stand a couple of good laughs. Stop being so serious, and start kidding around more. Seriously.

Reflections: Exercise 5

Which of the following is true for you?

____ I have an organized Rolodex of business and personal contacts.

____ I have an e-mail address book of business and personal contacts.

____ I make use of one of the above contacts by sending occasional e-mails or cards.

____ When I travel, I strike up conversation with people I sit next to on the plane.

____ I remember the names of people I am introduced to.

____ I also remember the name of the person who pours my coffee, fixes my car, serves me lunch, etc…

____ I have made at least one new contact in the last month.

Exercise 6

Lighten Up

Laughing your way to a healthier and more liberated existence

Summary

1. Humor is one of the most effective weapons you can use on a controlling person or environment. It empowers, provides an outlet for pent-up frustration and feelings of repression, and helps employees to detach from control.

2. A light-hearted approach helps to break the ice and establish a rapport between people of different cultural backgrounds in an increasingly multinational business climate.

3. A little leeway for on-the-job levity, viewed by some no-nonsense types as merely "goofing off," can actually help to build morale and employee loyalty and create a less stressed and more productive work force.

4. Medical research has shown that hearty laughter is a wonderful means of giving your body an "inner workout" and creating positive stress, which releases natural pain-killing endorphins and boosts the immune system. In other words, it helps keep you healthy.

5. By not taking anything that happens at work too seriously—the company could after all vanish overnight, as many have—you can make emotional detachment from the job that much easier.

"What I know for sure is that every day brings a chance for you to draw in a breath, kick off your shoes, and step out and dance—to live free of regret and filled with as much joy, fun and laughter as you can stand."
— *Oprah Winfrey*

A sense of humor is one of the most important attributes you need to break the hold of any command-and-control structure that might be dominating you or your fellow employees. When the day-to-day realities that you are observing seem to defy logical explanation, sometimes the only beneficial way left to respond is with laughter. You have to continue to put the day-to-day issues in the right context, and when you do there will always be an absurdity that will provide a laugh every day—especially in the corporate environment.

Humor is the one weapon you have for dealing with anyone who is trying to control you. Such an individual has no effective countermeasure—in fact, it is threatening and confusing to them. I will never forget sitting in a meeting with a very controlling CEO when one of the VPs started laughing at something going on between two people seated next to each other. When I saw his anger-driven- how-can-you-laugh-at-a-time-like-this response, I knew immediately that this guy had 'lost it'—that his appearance of being in control had been totally compromised. Laughter is a great uniting force—something that will help your morale and that of the people around you, as it is indeed contagious. Laughter will also help keep you healthy under stress, releasing positive endorphins, as medical studies have repeatedly shown. And the really great thing about humor is that it's the most effective means of supporting your emotional detachment, and thus essential for insulating yourself from actions based on fear and control.

How making a mockery of business led to a wild and crazy success story

By now, you've probably encountered so many absurd situations at work, you've lost count. You've no doubt heard the laments of colleagues—and perhaps have even indulged in a few yourself: "The way this company is set up is enough to drive anyone bananas," or "This office is an example of the inmates being put in charge of the asylum." To a young California bank employee, however, such corporate craziness wasn't simply a source of annoyance—it was a source of genuine inspiration. As he recalls, he first worked in "a number of humiliating and low paying jobs" before moving on to another bank where he worked in various technological and financial jobs that "defy description" (with a business card that identified him as an "engineer," even though he wasn't an engineer by training). All the while, however, he was busy observing the idiosyncrasies of his co-workers, on whom he based a doodle character that he used in business presentations. Eventually, on the advice of a cartoonist and following instructions in a book, he showed 50 sample cartoons to a syndicate, which accepted his idea for a comic strip based on his own work experiences. Thus was born "Dilbert," reflecting the daily frustrations and stupidities of corporate life.

But the strip's creator, Scott Adams, didn't quit his day job right then and there. He continued working at it for the next six or seven years, while devoting morning, evenings and weekends to doing the strip—no doubt providing himself with further inspiration and ammunition for his satire.

The result has been nothing less than phenomenal. What began as a little spoof on life at the office has gone on to become one of the most successful syndicated comic strips in the history of the funny pages. It has been picked up by approximately 2,000 newspapers in some 65 countries. Spin-offs have included four best-selling books written by Adams, two of which—*The Dilbert Principle* and *Dogbert's Top Secret Management Handbook*—were No. 1 on *The New York Times* Best Seller List. In addition, Dilbert has become the most widely read syndicated comic on the Internet.

In essence, the situations and characters depicted daily in Dilbert seem to have struck a universal chord of recognition among corporate employees the world over, providing a universal outlet for pent-up feelings of repression and resentment and converting them into a seemingly endless source of mirth instead. Rather than reacting to the obtuseness of their boss, the constrictions of corporate policies, and the controlling techniques of company brass with silent rage or a sense of helplessness, agitation, chagrin and humiliation, they had suddenly discovered that the things that bothered them most about their jobs were actually quite laughable. And any feelings they might have had of being somehow singled out for absurd or abusive treatment vanished, replaced by the realization that such experiences were nothing more than variations on the routines being played out as part of a widespread corporate farce. (Note: When I contacted Scott Adams to see if he was interested in collaborating on this book, he said that his function was mockery, not doing anything useful—a rather modest self-appraisal for someone whose work has been so universally useful in maintaining sanity in the workplace.)

The lesson is that humor genuinely empowers—and is especially effective as a means of breaking the psychological hold on employees that so many organizations seem to have, whether intentionally or not.

But helping you to detach from the emotional grip of fear and control isn't the only benefit of letting more levity into your life. A steady diet of laughter is increasingly regarded as one of the best ways you can keep yourself healthy, boost your immune system's ability to fight disease, and increase your mental sharpness (and that's no joke).

A belly laugh a day may just keep the doctor away

For many, many years, *Reader's Digest* has run some of its humorous anecdotes under the heading, "Laughter, the Best Medicine." That may originally have been intended as a mere metaphorical concept—but it turns out to have been right on the money from a scientific standpoint.

The individual credited with having "discovered" the therapeutic value of laughter in treating illness was *Saturday Review* editor Norman Cousins, who in 1964 was given a one-in-five-hundred chance of surviving a form of spinal disintegration with which he had been diagnosed (believed to be the result of heavy-metal poisoning). After reading about the negative effects of stress on the immune system, Cousins hypothesized that positive emotions could produce the opposite result. He later chronicled the entire episode in a book, *Anatomy of an Illness as Perceived by the Patient*, describing how he made it through the ordeal by abandoning the massive volume of painkillers he was being administered and medicating himself instead with daily doses of vitamin C and humor, spending hours immersed in the most uproariously funny things he could find—from Marx Brothers movies to an anthology of American humor that he had his nurse read to him. "I made the joyous discovery that ten minutes of genuine belly laughter had an anesthetic effect and would give me at least two hours of pain-free sleep," he noted.

Cousins not only managed to survive this seemingly terminal condition by using laughter as a remedy, but, perhaps even more astounding, got the usually skeptical medical community to give his unorthodox approach some serious attention. In addition to having part of his book published in the prestigious *New England Journal of Medicine* (and receiving responses from thousands of physicians) he was made a faculty member at the UCLA School of Medicine. He was also instrumental in the funding of studies that confirmed his theory about the healing value of hearty laughter, which he described in a subsequent book as a form of "internal jogging," with some of the same results as vigorous exercise.

In fact, given the pressures and demands faced by today's corporate employees, a good laugh or two could be just what the doctor ordered to help keep you both physically fit and mentally sharp—especially when you can't spare the time for a good walk or workout (although, as mentioned in Chapter 2, you should go out of your way to take an exercise break whenever possible). Its effects include increasing the oxygen supply to your blood and brain, releasing endorphins that are natural pain-relievers and produce a feeling of euphoria (similar to that of opiates, but with no side effects), and boosting the immune system.

The role of the funny bone in warding off disease has been substantiated by research on live and laughing subjects. In a paper entitled "The Laughter-Immune Connection," psychoneuroimmunologists (try pronouncing that!) Lee Berk and Stanley Tan, M.D., of Loma Linda University's Schools of Medicine and Public Health in California, described a study in which 10 medical students were hooked up to intravenous catheters, allowing blood samples to be taken before, during and after their viewing of a humorous video. Each of the samples showed a significant rise in inteferon-gamma (IFN), an immunoregulator produced by activated T cells and natural killer cells that fights viruses and, in the researchers' words, "serves to ensure cooperation between certain cells in the adaptive immune response."[11]

Such effects, according to Berk and Tan, are the result of "eustress," or beneficial stress, contrasted with negative stress, or distress (similar to the way "good" dietary fats are now differentiated from bad ones). Their research led them to the hypothesis that "mirthful laughter, a eustress effect, may produce beneficial health effects as the result of physiological and immunological changes."

As medical scientists, Berk and Tan also noted that they found it "gratifying and fulfilling to continue to discover objective scientific data to support beliefs that many have held intuitively for centuries, " citing Proverbs 17:22: "A merry heart doeth good like a medicine."

Beyond the physiological effects of laughter itself, however, there is another health benefit that derives from a lighthearted view of life. It's the relaxation response that comes with the ability to not take anything that happens in your job all that seriously—using your sense of humor as another way of detaching from both control and results.

Not too long ago, I did consulting work for a company with a management team that was a lot of fun to work with, despite a very controlling CEO. Once the laughter started within this group, it was unstoppable. One time, in a more serious moment, a group of us reflected on what would happen to the industry if the company didn't exist. The answer was nothing. Competitors would soon suck up the market share, and consumers would barely know the difference. When you put it in those terms, then reflect on the sense of gravity that imbues corporate meetings, you can't help but laugh at the undue importance we attach to business affairs. Think for a moment about the number of companies that no longer exist today—Eastern Airlines, Studebaker-Packard, Pan Am, Pet.com, and many others, much like the legions of small enterprises that fold every year. Yet had you attended their meetings, you probably would have thought the world revolved around their activities.

To quote Dr. Meyer Friedman, author of *Treating Type A Behavior and Your Heart,* "The person most effectively protecting himself against the continued progress of coronary artery disease is the person willing to see himself and his affairs as ludicrously unimportant in the planetary scheme of things."

In essence, then, laughter will not only serve to neutralize the "controller," but will help you physically and mentally as well. What a great antidote to the stress that the controlling environment will try to engender in you!

'Cracking up' the ice between corporate cultures

It's been observed that what might strike people in one country as hilarious falls flat when repeated to people in another—they just don't get it. But that can also work in reverse when something that's not intended to be funny becomes hilarious once it crosses the cultural barrier

I had a chance to observe this first-hand back around 1990 when I was selling a company called Pacific Basin Foods to a Japanese corporation. On this particular occasion, the U.S. company's management team had been assembled to meet with the Japanese company's top brass for an explanation of the principles, values and codes of conduct that guided the latter company. The CEO of the Japanese firm was there with interpreters on both sides of him. Now, I knew for a fact that this gentleman was proficient in English because he had used it at previous meetings I had had with him, where a translator was present only for the purpose of clarification. But most of this particular management group had never met with him personally, and he apparently preferred that the relationship remain somewhat impersonal and remote, a purpose well served by maintaining a language barrier. So at this gathering he spoke no English, but depended on his interpreters to communicate with the managers and tell them about his company's strong work ethic—one that included some very long hours. Not that the members of the team need be concerned about how their spouses might react to this disconcerting news, however, because the company had devised a way of taking care of that problem. At the end of the year, they were told, each would be given a "special wife bonus".

When I heard this utterly absurd proposition, the last thing I wanted to do was start cracking up. So I started focusing very hard on a spot on the ceiling, trying to keep my chortles in check and everything "quite correct." But just then one of the managers (who at this point had apparently begun to have some apprehension over just how much their new Japanese bosses expected of them) raised his hand and, like a scene out of a Dilbert strip, asked, "Can you explain this 'wife bonus?'" before starting to giggle. As soon as that happened, the entire management team lost it, and everyone was soon in stitches. It was obvious that the Japanese really didn't understand what it was that struck them all so funny, and how foolish we thought they were. But what was even funnier was that they all started spontaneously laughing, too—including the CEO—seeming to enjoy the jocularity at their expense. And it proved to be a real ice-breaker—one that led to a good enough working relationship to keep all the key employees of Pacific Basin Foods on board for at least another decade—and never did the "wife bonus" come up again.

Of course, some people who believe in being politically correct might counsel those so affected to stifle their reaction lest they show disrespect for whatever protocol might prevail in such a situation, particularly when it involves dealing with controlling corporate business interests run by foreigners. But in a corporate culture that, for better or worse, has become increasingly multinational, a light-hearted approach is sometimes just what's needed to break the ice and make people more comfortable with each other.

How 'comic relief' from stress can make you more productive

What the above anecdote also illustrates (as if we needed any further evidence) is that laughter is contagious and the perfect neutralizer for many controlling situations. And because it spreads so easily, it doesn't take much of it to loosen up the atmosphere of even the most tightly controlled office.

I've seen several examples of how a little humor interjected into the routine can transform such organizations by transforming people. One occurred on my third day at a company whose chairman I had just replaced on my way to becoming CEO. Both the president of the company, whom I'll call Jim, and the executive vice president who had an office next to his were quintessential corporate men who believed in running the proverbial "tight ship" (a management style I thought somewhat incongruous for an outfit whose products and image were strictly "New Age"). As a result, the administrative group who worked just outside of these offices always seemed very somber and quiet. The place was so quiet, in fact, that it bothered me. So one day, when I walked in and noticed a stereo next to one of the support group desks, I turned it on, not too loud, but loud enough for the music to fill the immediate area. The president promptly emerged and blew his top, thinking that one of two employees who sat in the immediate area had had the audacity to turn it on. They didn't say a word when I came out of my office but when Jim returned to his, all three of us burst out laughing, and in no time the levity had spread to the accounting group stationed nearby. The president, in essence, had been neutralized by laughter—and from that point on not only was music a must in the office, but laughter was a common occurrence, especially when someone made himself or herself into fair game by indulging in decidedly stern or stuffy behavior.

Such antics are in keeping with a burgeoning movement toward creating a less oppressive working environment—one that emphasizes "learning to lighten up on the job—to take yourself lightly while continuing to take your work seriously, " in the words of Paul E. McGhee, Ph.D. "Your sense of humor is one of the most powerful tools you have for coping with any source of stress in your life," he observes in an article posted on his Web site, *The Laughter Remedy.* "When you're able to find a light side of deadlines, conflicts and other aspects of your job—especially on the tough days—you have a tool for letting go of the frustrations and upsets of the moment. This enables you to sustain a frame of mind conducive to dealing more effectively with the problem of the moment." And that significantly contributes to "increased productivity and quality service," says McGhee, who is among a growing number of entrepreneurs specializing in providing companies with programs designed to give the workplace a cheerier atmosphere and provide a measure of 'comic relief' from stress.[9]

Of course, there are those "no-nonsense types"—and you've undoubtedly dealt with them—who continue to believe that levity somehow undermines the work ethic and is generally counterproductive. But such autocrats of the office scene are 'seriously' behind the times, stubbornly resisting what has by now become quite obvious to most behavioral experts and is becoming more and more apparent to many organizations—that happier people make better workers, and that merriment and morale are closely interrelated.

"There's an assumption that if employees are having a good time and laughing, then they're goofing off," notes Terrill Fischer, dean of humor at "Humor University," a business training and consulting firm in Austin, Texas. "The important question that must be answered is: Is the work being done? If it is, then what does it matter if the people doing the work are having a good time?"[10]

Recently, I have been quite impressed with Albertson's CEO Larry Johnson, who has hired Ed Foreman to work with the employees of Albertson's at all levels of the company. Foreman is a tremendous motivational speaker who basically says life is not for working, worrying or whining, but for loving, living and laughing. How many CEOs would pay someone a lot of money to tell their employees that working and worrying are not the main purpose of life?

An affinity for frivolity: the real way to win friends and influence employees

To some natural-born killjoys, however, the issue isn't whether the work is being done, but rather whether the office is an appropriate setting to appear to be having fun. Laughter and lightheartedness on the job, they'll tell you, detracts from doing business in a dignified manner, and doesn't show the proper respect for one's employer. What bothers such people is the idea that a somewhat irreverent atmosphere might have the effect of emancipating employees from their control.

Not that their concerns are entirely baseless—it is difficult, after all, to dominate a group of people who are generally in high spirits and always ready to snicker when something strikes them as funny. Laughter, in that respect, is indeed liberating. But what they always fail to take into consideration is that a stick-in-the-mud seldom commands real loyalty or respect of the kind that motivates people to put forth their best efforts—and that the manager who behaves in an uptight or authoritarian manner simply ends up alienating subordinates and making himself or herself the object of whispered ridicule. On the other hand, the boss who gives his workers a little leeway to be themselves and let off steam usually doesn't have to be unduly demanding to get the desired results.

Perhaps if such 'deskpots' got to the movies more often (like the CEO I mentioned in Excercise 2 who spent his lunch breaks at the cinema), or at least rented more videos, they would be more aware of how often this message has been played out on the wide screen—particularly in films with military settings. From classics like "Mister Roberts," in which a happy-go-lucky officer on board a Navy ship in World War II succeeds in undermining the command of its curmudgeonly captain, to Robin Williams' depiction in "Good Morning, Vietnam" of wise-cracking

Armed Forces Radio disc jockey Adrian Croneaur whose on-air defiance of his humor-challenged superior turns him into an icon among the combat troops, it's the fun-loving individual who always manages to win people's hearts and minds.

For living proof of how that principle applies to business, Fischer cites the example of Southwest Airlines, a highly profitable operation for more than a quarter century—and whose chairman and CEO, Herb Kelleher, has adopted a "philosophy of fun." To quote Kelleher (who has made public appearances in Easter Bunny and Elvis get-ups), "Who says a lighthearted approach to business is incompatible with success?"

"By welcoming laughter and fun," Fischer observed, "he also has opened his arms to ambition, initiative, high morale, high productivity and low turnover among Southwest employees, along with incredible loyalty among customers."

I recently flew Southwest and saw this for myself. Efficiency and humor—what a combination! The turnaround time from when my plane came in until we boarded was remarkable—three times as fast as the major airlines. And while it was boarding, the flight attendant was on the PA system joking about individual carry-on baggage. This was truly refreshing in comparison to the long turnaround and grim faces on the major full-service airlines I usually fly.

A slightly frivolous approach can also go a long way toward keeping things in an organization more above-board—a phenomenon I myself have witnessed on a number of occasions. I can recall a particular board meeting of a public company at which some particularly sensitive issues were due to be addressed, including the matter of this firm possibly being acquired by a larger corporation. But what chiefly concerned the management group was the CEO's increasingly disengaged attitude toward company affairs, and, even more disconcerting, his having ordered one of the group's members to make a presentation to the board that the managers all knew was deliberately misleading about this acquisition.

It was in this climate of doubt that the management group met in its own private session prior to making its presentations to the board. The subject of the perfidious presentation had just arisen when one of the managers looked over at a colleague and put his finger on his nose then made a gesture to signify his nose growing, like Pinocchio's did whenever he told a fib. The rest of the group did likewise, and immediately began roaring with laughter. But the joke didn't end there. For the duration of that meeting, the management group assumed the secret subversive identity of "Pinocchio Partners"—with one senior vice president even proclaiming himself Gepetto—and resolved to clandestinely make mock of the disingenuous CEO-mandated report by sitting at the back of the room and threatening to give the person delivering it the "nose finger" whenever it seemed appropriate.

Not only did this serve to dispel the tension that the situation had created for the managers, it ultimately gave the individual making the misleading presentation the courage to clarify the true state of affairs to the chairman of the board (yes, this person was in fact me). What had begun as a bit of clowning had evolved into candor—attributes that could go a long way toward redeeming public trust in some of today's corporations.

Levity can also help resolve conflicts within an organization that can often be counterproductive. Fischer gives the example of a workshop his firm ran in which the managers of a particular company were asked to work up a short sketch on the organization's culture. "One group sat there and argued, and their people even walked off," he recalled. "Then someone said, 'Wait a minute. This is how we behave around here. This is our culture.'

"The managers then put together a humorous skit about the time they ruined an annual company celebration with infighting. People were rolling in the aisles. This opened up communication channels and helped heal the scars around this event."

There is the special power that a smile, an easy laugh and a congenial personality have in inspiring an aura of trust and confidence. Happy people are individuals whom others like to be around—and to whom others look for balance and perspective. Perhaps that's one reason why McGhee has had companies tell him that in filling many new positions—especially managerial ones—they look for evidence of a sense of humor in an applicant. "They know that this is a skill that will serve both the employee and the company well," he noted.

OK, now—all set for your next 'assignment?'

Let's step back a moment and see how far you've come since starting on these exercises. You have a firm grip on your mission, you're becoming healthier and more versatile every day, you have faced up to the 'controller' and declared your psychological independence, detached from results, formed a network of new (and old) contacts, and learned to laugh at the absurdity of the entire scenario. Now you're ready to take the last step toward survival in a corporate culture, and share the benefits of what you've learned and experienced with others.

Reflections: Exercise 6

Think about the last tense situation you encountered at work. Was it alleviated any by humor?

_____

_____

_____

_____

_____

_____

Think of something, even something small, you might do to 'lighten things up' at work. You need not be in a management position to inject some fun into the atmosphere of your workplace (although if you are, that's even better).

_____

_____

_____

_____

_____

_____

When was the last time you laughed until you cried? What makes you laugh? What movies make you laugh? Books? Friends?

_____

_____

_____

_____

_____

_____

Exercise 7

Share Your Experience

Mentoring and other means of providing mutual reinforcement

Summary

1. Learn to appreciate how exchanging information based on personal knowledge and experience with your coworkers can serve as a form of mutual support against fear-and-control-based management techniques.

2. Make it part of your personal mission to mentor a new recruit in your organization or department. The benefits can include reinforcing your own expertise and reputation, building a foundation of trust, enhancing your 'people options,' learning from the person being mentored, the satisfaction of helping someone to succeed, and helping carry on an important tradition.

3. To find someone to mentor, be sure to make yourself open, accessible and helpful to recent hires—but be aware that mentoring relationships don't always begin on a smooth note.

4. Be ready and willing to accept mentoring yourself, even at an advanced stage in your career. Recognize that there's always someone "older and wiser"—and you should never give up the search for wisdom.

5. Make it a point to exchange knowledge and experience with contemporaries in your office as well, realizing just how important it can be to look to others for support. And don't make the mistake of ignoring solutions that come from people in lower echelons of the organization.

6. Share the process of making positive life changes with your domestic partner.

*"The older I get, the greater power I seem to have to help the world;
I am like a snowball—the further I am rolled the more I gain."*
— *Susan B. Anthony*

Now that you're armed with the tools to reclaim your power and neutralize the effects of working in a fear-and-control-based corporate culture, you should be feeling happier, healthier, and more productive at work. So how can you use your knowledge to benefit someone else?

The most effective way is to mentor someone—a process that will help you as well as another person by reinforcing the skills you've learned and acquired. Beyond that, every day you should act as a cheerleader—one who constantly strives to reinforce the morale of your colleagues, share your experiences with them, lighten their unconscious load, and release them from the bonds of control as well.

Corporate rip currents—and how you can help others to swim free of them

The unseen, faceless corporate culture has a way of somehow sucking people in. Getting pulled into fear-and-control dramas over a paycheck can be very much like getting caught up in a "rip tide." One of these treacherous currents can easily drag you out to sea no matter how hard or desperately you try to swim back—that is, unless you realize that all you have to do is swim sideways out of its narrow but powerful grip. Once you've succeeded in doing that, getting back to shore can be relatively easy. Had only such knowledge been shared with more people in past years, it could easily have prevented many drowning deaths

By the same token, it's time for you to get busy helping fellow workers learn the survival strategies of which you're now in possession—and a good starting place is wherever and whenever you see people trying to swim against the corporate current. Empathize with them and explain why you are now smiling and feeling better about things. Have you ignored or given the brush-off to someone who is trying to be your friend? Then open yourself up to that person and teach them what you have learned—and you will be amazed at what they'll teach you in the process. There will be instant recognition on your part of the persistent pain and stress they are experiencing, while they will recognize the fact that for whatever reason, you are no longer carrying a burden. Such mutual understanding will be contagious, helping you to acquire additional expertise in your field, develop more networking connections, and build bridges to your fellow workers. Your newfound tools—your personal mission, reclaiming the time that belongs to you,

detaching from control and results, networking and laughing more—are
waiting to be shared.

My desire to share what I've learned was, in fact, what led to the
writing of this book—and these exercises are among the things you can
share with your teammates to help them navigate those treacherous corporate currents.

Mutual support and enlightenment
—an antidote to corporate control

"The healthy human response is ... to do what children do. Reach
to others for support," advises Robert Maurer, a Ph.D. and clinical
psychologist at the UCLA School of Medicine. Men who do so live
longer, have lower cholesterol, are more likely to endure crises without
becoming ill, and make more effective leaders," Maurer observed in a
magazine article on dealing with fear that we often interpret as stress.
"So the next time you're feeling stressed," he urges, "do two things:
identify your fear, and find people who can help you deal with it."[12]

It's not just the individual employee who can benefit from the load-
lightening effects of such exchanges, however. Companies themselves
would do well to be guided by the experience and accumulated wisdom
of the people who work for them—and I don't mean just those on upper-
management levels whose vision is often clouded by their own agendas. The
value of having those in the trenches brought in on the decision-making
process is something that has become obvious to more enlightened firms—
but is still largely lost in our top-heavy corporate culture.

I had a chance to observe this first-hand a few years ago when I was
called in to try to rescue a $300 million food service distribution com-
pany whose fortunes, due to various factors, were on a downhill slide.
This firm was losing money at the rate of about a million dollars a
month. When I arrived, I not only found a tremendous amount of
excess—the computer system alone could have been used for a company ten times larger—I realized immediately that its senior management
was largely clueless and out of touch. What really interested me, however, was the untapped amount of practical understanding possessed by
the lower-level employees with whom I met, and their desire to make a
difference. It was the management layer separating them and me that
was the problem.

I'll never forget this one meeting I had with several hundred workers
at the largest distribution center, which took place in the center of a ware-
house. After dismissing all the senior officers (which made them extremely

uncomfortable), I stood together with the employees on a stack of pallets and proceeded to have an amazingly positive and constructive discussion with them. I found it so eye-opening, in fact, that I went on the road and held similar meetings with the employees at the company's other distribution centers. I also met privately with the head of the union—this was a Teamsters local with very stringent work rules—and discovered him to be a very knowledgeable individual who really was dedicated to the welfare of his membership and not unreasonable at all.

It was amazing to watch the way those employees rallied and improved things once they were empowered, making changes that amounted to about $700,000 in savings a month. And while it may not have been enough to put the company back in the black, it was truly a revelation—one that made me realize just how much corporations might profit by allowing those who haven't made it to the top to share the benefits of the experience and perspective they've gained outside the executive suite. Through this experience several hourly workers became friends, I learned a tremendous amount from them, and, God willing, they learned something from me as well. These relationships were what made this very difficult turnaround a wonderful experience.

If you're in corporate management, here would be my addendum to Dr. Maurer's advice: when you do feel the need to reach out to others for support, and to find people to help you deal with things, don't just rely on those who might be on the same rung of the success ladder. Try looking "below and beyond" your status level as well. Remember: the wise counsel you seek is far more likely to be found on the factory floor than on the proverbial mountaintop.

Mentoring: a means of empowering both yourself and others

A number of years ago, a college senior read a book called *The Intelligent Investor,* which so impressed him that he decided to pursue his Master's degree in Economics at Columbia University where its author, Benjamin Graham, taught a business course. Three years after graduating, he finally managed to land a job with Graham's investment firm. After spending another two years being personally mentored by Graham, the former student returned to his home town of Omaha, Nebraska, and with seven investors and a mere $100 of his own, launched an investment firm that within five years would make him a millionaire.

Warren Buffett was well on his way to becoming the country's second richest man—due in no small measure to the intelligent investment strategies he learned from an eminent expert who saw his potential and found the time to mentor him.[13] In return, Warren Buffett has mentored

America's wealthiest individual, Bill Gates. Mentoring is an instinctual way of giving back and receiving more in return.

Such is the power of mentoring—a form of personal philanthropy that you can easily make part of your mission in life. You do not have to be famous at what you do to become a mentor. All it takes is enough experience in your craft or profession and a willingness to share your expertise and understanding with a "rookie" in your organization or department.

To the latter, of course, the benefits of such guidance can be considerable. As popular business author Robert G. Allen notes, the advantages a mentor offers include perspective—"the wisdom of a lifetime of experience," proficiency—simplifying the learning process while helping the pupil to avoid the pitfalls and "hard knocks," and training in being patient.[14] Many of our most notable achievers, in fact, credit their success to the influence of one or more mentors on their careers. But what, you may wonder, is in it for you as the person doing the mentoring?

The answer is: more than you might have imagined. There are few business-related activities, in fact, that are likely to be quite as personally and professionally rewarding as providing instruction, insight and inspiration to an entry-level colleague. For it is through the act—and art—of mentoring that our connections and interaction with others reach their highest levels, enabling us to forge mutually beneficial relationships that are likely to be a source of satisfaction, self-affirmation, expanded awareness, gratitude and solidarity against corporate domination for many years to come.

How, precisely, do you yourself gain from guiding others in this manner? Let us count the ways:

- Teaching someone else the ropes in your particular area of expertise tends to reinforce your own sense of mastery over what you do—and to revitalize your feeling of authority and control that corporate culture is so often apt to undermine.

- Coaching an individual perhaps half your age can be as educational an experience for you as for them. I find it absolutely fascinating how when I mentor someone 20 years younger than me, just how much I learn from that individual—and how much new energy I pick up from them. They may think they're doing all the learning, but in a sense I'm also being mentored in the different way they have of looking at things—especially in a world that's so different from that of a generation or two ago. (I am especially impressed with today's 25-to-35 age group—they seem so much bolder and willing to try something different than I was at that age.)

- Sharing your know-how and experience with others in the company helps to establish a climate of respect and esteem for your exploits and accomplishments, transforming your image from that of an "older worker" to a "seasoned veteran."

- Mentoring helps build a foundation of trust. In fact, for someone working in a higher executive echelon, a willingness to personally break in or train people can be especially important as a way of gaining the confidence of those on a lower rung with whom interaction might otherwise be difficult. (On one occasion, for instance, my mentoring activities as a CEO led to my being privately informed of an employee's copying of confidential records.) By causing others to view you in a new light, the process can significantly increase your ability as a manager to understand the dynamics that exist on different staff levels, and to help break down the psychological barriers that allow the corporation to maintain a controlling environment.

- The individuals with whom you share your knowledge and experience will be among your most valued and meaningful "people options." Providing someone with personal training, sage advice, and encouragement at a crucial time in their life and career is likely to give them a very special place in your circle of relationships, and vice versa. And you never know at what point such connections may unexpectedly prove instrumental in advancing your own fortunes (see box, page 141) or otherwise enhancing your life (as was illustrated in the anecdote in Exercise 5 about Jacob Liebglid, who started the youthful Samuel Goldwyn in the glove-making trade that enabled him to survive and prosper after his arrival in America).

- Mentoring begets mentoring, and thus makes you a vital link in a chain of influence—a significant player in a sort of "pay-it-forward" tradition of perpetuating both professional proficiency and good will in your field of endeavor.

- Who knows? Perhaps, as was the case with Warren Buffett, you may have helped start someone down the road not just to success, but fame and glory as well—and should that occur, you'll have the satisfaction (and perhaps even the recognition) of having played a significant role in it.

In essence, mentoring is like building your own personal savings account of good will, gratitude, reinforcement and recognition. And those are the kinds of assets that not even the most lucrative 401K or stock portfolio can provide you with.

And, above all (returning once again to the message conveyed in that comedy of corporate morality, *The Apartment*), becoming a mentor is one of the best ways you can prove that you're a mensch.

Opening the door to a mentoring relationship

How, exactly, does one go about forming a mentoring relationship in a company? I would say the first step is to smile, be friendly and helpful—go out of your way to chat with new people, answer questions, and perhaps even volunteer to help train probationary employees. Once you've made yourself accessible, you may not have to find a particular individual to mentor, since the person is likely to seek you out. One day, for instance, someone may approach you requesting assistance in some particular area of their job, setting the stage for you to help them in other ways. Or a person just starting out with the organization might open up an opportunity for rapport with some leading question, like "How long have you been with the company," or "How do you manage to do all that in one day?" Such an overture could well be an indicator that you've come upon a likely candidate for mentoring. In fact, you should give a sign that you are willing to help. If you see a group of new or young employees, find something about one of them on which to base a positive comment. They will be surprised to find you so approachable and in all likelihood will seek you out for advice or guidance.

Over the course of my career, I have mentored several individuals who picked me in this manner, rather than the other way around. That's not to say there won't be occasions when you'd like to offer unsolicited advice to a relative newcomer, or someone in a lower tier of the company. When that happens, stop for a moment and ask yourself honestly whether the impulse is from the heart, or if you have any sort of ulterior motive in wanting to do so—for instance, some type of resentment or grudge you might be harboring that might cause you to want to take this individual down a peg. If you do indeed have such a "hidden agenda," it's probably best to keep your suggestions to yourself. But If your inclination to take the person aside is based on a sincere desire to offer them the benefit of your guidance, in all probability it will resonate with them, and may well open the door to your becoming their mentor.

It goes without saying, of course, that the individual you're most likely to end up mentoring will be a younger coworker within the same organization, given that you'll already have a workplace, corporate culture and professional language in common. But even that doesn't necessarily have to be the case.

On one occasion, for instance, I became involved in counseling a young Wharton graduate who had unsuccessfully sought a position with a firm for whom I did some consulting work. As we talked, it became evident that the real reason he wanted a job was to heal his bruised ego following the failure of an entrepreneurial venture. He had not only lost both his money and that of other investors, but his nerve for going into business as well. In fact, he had another enterprise in mind—one that sounded rather promising—but was scared to death of failing again. Having had my share of both failures and successes, I discussed the pros and cons with him at some length. Today, he is back in business, seems to be doing well, is networking with many people, and is rather excited about his future prospects. And while I can't exactly take credit for all that, I like to believe the perspective and encouragement I provided him was instrumental in his decision to persevere. That's why I believe that one should never underestimate the degree of help that just talking to someone can give them—especially if you have valuable experience in their field or a related one.

The thing I like best about mentoring someone in this manner is that I am also reinforcing my own resolve in the process. I am, in effect, reminding myself of all the things I've learned over the course of my career that I might be inclined to forget if I wasn't passing them on to someone else—including the tools for staying independent in outlook, emotionally objective, and physically healthy. They need to be honed and oiled every day, and showing a colleague how to use them is one of the best ways to achieve that. The same goes for sharing your experiences—what management guru Stephen Covey, author of *Seven Habits of Successful People*, would call "sharpening the saw." The mutual respect and sense of trust that these relationships foster is invaluable. In addition, there is a great feeling of accomplishment that mentoring—and even being mentored –produces. Revisiting my career is always a great reminder of how much I still have to learn.

Remember, too, that mentoring within your own corporation is perhaps the most effective thing you can do to change its culture from within. In fact, it is just about the only way. Imagine everyone in the office smiling, laughing and being extremely productive. No backbiting, just trust. Communication between people becomes smoother because it's more direct, devoid of politics or hidden agendas.

Change begins with the people—and once they start to think for themselves, it can't help but diminish the effectiveness of the fear-and-control tactics used by authority figures. That could eventually lead to "central command" having to relinquish much of its power over them, causing the entire structure to change as a result.

An example of what can happen once mentoring sets the ball in motion

Gil Patterson's future couldn't have looked more promising at the start of 1977. Having just begun his major-league career as a pitcher for the New York Yankees, he was already considered to be the best young right-hander in baseball.But just 10 games into his first season, he was sidelined by arm injuries which effectively scuttled his ball-playing ambitions, despite eight operations, his learning to pitch left-handed, and seven years of trying to make a comeback.

Finally, he began coaching for the minor leagues—only to lose that job when, as ESPN's Keith Olbermann noted in a recent commentary on the game, "his bosses thought he was coddling the young pitchers in his charge." After that, he spent seven years coaching teenagers in public parks in Florida, and another 10 years doing further coaching in the minors.

But then, a job for a pitching coach opened up on the Toronto Blue Jays, and Al Leiter of the New York Mets called the team and recommended the coach who had been accused of "coddling" him back in 1984 for the position.

Patterson got the job—something that probably never would have happened had his mentoring not left such a positive and lasting impression.

Simply being older and wiser doesn't mean you're past being mentored

To mentor someone is to be a link in a chain of influence. In this book, for instance, you have just acquired a set of skills to help you thrive in a corporate culture. There can be no better way to help a fellow employee than to pass them on.

Whatever ability I have to counsel those starting out today, in fact, is something I owe to the training I received from my own mentors, beginning with my upbringing. Yes, it is possible for one's parents to also be one's mentors, and I was fortunate to have had two outstanding, loving parents in this regard whose influence I credit with having instilled in me a "can-do" spirit. My father was a very hard-working fisherman and my mother ran the household, and both of them had a positive way of always pushing me to new levels of accomplishment in school and in sports, convincing me that I was capable of going farther than I ever imagined. It was a great gift that I will always cherish. In fact, if there were official role models who personified parental mentoring skills, I would nominate my parents.

I have some great memories of various people in companies I worked for taking me under their wing at just the right times, when such guidance was crucial to my ability to perform (and who I believe are deserving of personal recognition, as are all mentors who make a difference in our lives). Very early in my career—right out of college, in fact—I was fortunate enough to have not one, but three individuals who made sure I made a smooth transition into the corporate world. It was at Foodmaker, my first employer in the food industry, that I met this particular trio of mentors—Gene Dennis, Danny Spinnazola and Dave Boynton. They saw to it that I got opportunities to prove my mettle, making as few mistakes as possible, and they guided me as to what was important. In fact, when the company wanted to move me to Houston and I declined, they covered my butt in what for anyone else could have been a career-ending decision. Later, when I arrived at Ralston Purina, individuals like Davis McCarty and Ed McMillan sheltered me from many of the issues that typically make young people in a company cower or become discouraged. They were always there for me, through my good times and tough ones. Without these early mentors, I'm convinced I would never have developed the confidence I have today. One time, through a reorganization, I was given a new boss who was a real "hard ass" and I was afraid he was going to suffocate me. But David and Ed worked their magic, and before the ink on the reorganization had dried, I was reporting to Ed. Thank God for mentors!

But just because I'm older and somewhat wiser now doesn't mean I've stopped imbibing wisdom from others. Despite the fact that we might go on to become mentors ourselves, I like to think that we never outgrow our need for mentoring—even though it might take somewhat different forms in our later years.

There was, for instance, the time back in 1995 that I was sitting in a cigar lounge with my buddy from the Bubba Gump Shrimp Company, Kenny Lee, when we encountered a public relations executive from New York named Sol Zatt. Sol was an 84-year-old in-your-face kind of guy with a manner that was decidedly undiplomatic. When he asked me about what I did and I told him a little about my work as a consultant, he had no qualms about making me feel foolish on several counts. Now I'll admit I was somewhat shaken at first, but I also recognized that he might have a point or two—and instead of taking offense, I realized the advice, however abrasively offered, could prove to be quite helpful. In fact, I wanted to know more.

As a result, I've made a point of adding Sol to my collection of connections –and in the years since, he's continued to get in my face and has helped me to be much more forthcoming about issues than I ever thought I could be. Sol also taught me a valuable lesson for which I will always thank him: that if clients are really serious about needing your skills, they will pay you twice as much as you think they're willing to—but you have only one shot at getting it, so don't be shy when it comes to negotiating a fee. I have continued to use Sol's advice, and I've found out that it does indeed work.

I should note that throughout my career, I have made it a point to find people to emulate and study. For many years, the person who most inspired me—you might call him my virtual mentor—was Jack Welch, the now retired and always outspoken CEO of General Electric, whose views on business are reflected in his book *Straight from the Gut*. I was particularly enamored of his no-boundaries philosophy of accepting ideas from everywhere and "eliminating bureaucracy and all the nonsense that comes with it by empowering the people in the organization," and would often attempt to use it as a guidepost in my own business dealings. (In fact, the source of that quote—a letter from a GE annual report—has been in one of my to-do binders for at least 20 years). But in trying to understand what it takes to build a great organization, I came around to the realization that not all of his ideas were necessarily applicable to me.

Then I read a book called *The Chaordic Age*, and for the first time I felt thoroughly enlightened, my vision clarified, the gaps in my understanding filled in. It's the story of how Dee Hock, one-time vice president of a Seattle-based bank, went on to create the world's largest corporation, Visa International. I was tremendously impressed with the book and the concept it conveyed of having a group of people working to achieve a common mission because it involves specific principles and values in which they all share a belief. To me, it represented a repudiation of the corporate command- and-control ethic that has created such a repressive workplace environment. It also got me wondering whether such a system could be utilized to correct some of the root problems that have made American agriculture and other institutions increasingly less viable. But it took my wife Lisa to orchestrate the event that would enable me to start turning mere theorizing into action.

The occasion was my 47th birthday, and she had arranged for us to fly to Seattle for what she promised would be a big surprise. Of course, I knew what it would be—a salmon-fishing excursion that I wasn't really all that excited about at the time, but for which I had practiced sounding enthusiastic. As it turned out, I was wrong. The surprise was a meeting with Dee Hock himself—one that began at 11 a.m. and ended up lasting until 4:30 in the afternoon. I must admit I was totally overwhelmed, finding him to be even more inspiring in person than in his book. In fact, he inspired me to get together with a group of associates and launch an agricultural analogue to Visa called Family Farm brand—a venture whose mission is to use common principles and values to create a more viable and consumer-friendly agricultural production and distribution system. By building an enterprise limited to, and operated by, family farms, rather than those run by agribusiness interests, we believe we can provide healthier and more economical commodities to the public while rejuvenating rural communities and helping to save the environment. It may sound like an ambitious undertaking, but we've already got a group of people on board who are experts at making things happen—individuals with a variety of skills who have translated the inspiration provided by Dee Hock into a real working model. And Dee continues to be a consultant. In fact, I have followed up our initial meeting to personally sit with him and review where we are, and listen to his perspective and streams of wisdom (on which it sometimes seem I can't take notes fast enough). And his son Steve is helping us write the bylaws and constitution. Whenever I leave these meetings, I feel ready to conquer the world—or at least, change the face of American agriculture.

If we do indeed succeed in our goals of saving family farms and making America a healthier country in the process, I'll have my own personal mentor (and my wife) to thank. I'll also have to include in my acknowledgments the influence that books have had on my life—and although I may not end up as rich as Warren Buffett as a result, I know I'll feel every bit as richly rewarded. I personally believe that the mentoring process is not optional but essential. Every time I reach a juncture in my career, I look for a mentor. Recently, for instance, I have been very fortunate to have been mentored by Bob Samuels, who is a straightforward, no-nonsense individual with incredible insight into people and business organizations and whom I think of as having virtually reinvented integrity and honesty in business. I have also recently picked up a tremendous amount of new understanding from a true Renaissance man, Bill Nicholson. I can't help but feel that these relationships will one day result in my having much more to write about.

The critical importance of sharing experiences with your partner

Whenever you go about making significant change in your life, it usually is going to require some help—or at least moral support—from those closest to you. It's also apt to have an impact on their lives. Quitting smoking, for example, is certainly in everyone's best interest—especially yourself and your family. By the same token, it is also likely to have the effect of making you irritable and more difficult to get along with for however long it takes you to lose your dependence on the evil weed.

The seven exercises recommended here can also be life-altering—in fact, they're meant to be (although hopefully without the producing the side effects of tobacco withdrawal). So if, after reading this book, you think they just might change your life for the better and are serious about giving all or any one of them a try (and that includes being serious about lightening up, which can be especially challenging if you're in the process of giving up smoking), you should by all means share that intent with your spouse, life partner or significant other. The perspective that a spouse often brings to such a metamorphosis can be truly amazing.

My wife Lisa has been especially helpful in my being able to successfully shed the shackles of corporate control. When we were first married, I was a confirmed workaholic—so dedicated to my corporate job responsibilities that everything else in my life was relegated to second or third place (or sometimes no place at all). I was so driven, in fact, that I literally didn't have time to drive—gladly letting Lisa do all the driving while I caught up on my trade publications. She and I worked at the same company in those days, so we were both totally preoccupied with work, briefly finding a chance to cut loose by getting together with friends over cocktails on Friday evenings.

When we both decided that this was not the lifestyle we wanted and that one stressed-out person was enough, we decided it would be best for Lisa to quit her job and pursue other options—even though it would impact us financially. Once she was able to clear her head, it became obvious to her that I was way too consumed by work. She kept pointing out to me how little I was really getting out of my supercharged existence. Slowly, I began to realize how the corporation had taken control of my entire life. It was an evolution in my thinking that eventually led to the writing of this book—and, once again, as in the case of my becoming allied with Dee Hock, I have Lisa to thank for setting the wheels in motion. In fact, she remains an integral part of my maintenance plan, seeing to it that the companies for whom I now consult don't sneakily suck me into their control dramas.

Once you've changed course, you may be surprised to learn just how wearing it was on the person who loves you more than anyone else to hear your constant, unremitting complaints about your controlling boss. What makes it particularly important to include your partner in the process is that as you go through these exercises, you will be taking time to look at things you have been too busy or preoccupied to pay attention to before. One of those things is going to be the quality of your personal relationships, not only with your spouse or significant other, but with family members and friends. All of a sudden, you will begin to see such relationships with new eyes—and you may discover that you have drifted so far apart from those you value most that acknowledging it could be a somewhat painful experience. My wife and I both know many couples whose relationships have suffered from such work-related neglect, but who have never taken time to analyze the problem. Again, like quitting smoking, these are life changes that have positive results but are not easy to accomplish without support. Beyond the reinforcement you receive from your peers and from mentoring someone, make sure you involve your partner in the process.

Keep in mind, however, that this shouldn't be merely a one-sided transition you'll be making. Sharing these exercises also means that your partner should closely examine the effect of his or her work on your relationship. When one person moves ahead through enlightened self-discovery but his or her partner remains stuck in a rut due to complacency or fear of change, it can sometimes destroy a relationship. The effect will be more profound and healing if you go through it together. Growing together is fun and challenging—it helps each to enjoy the process more, and can genuinely revitalize a relationship that's growing stale. And there are many things you can do to reinforce such mutual growth—for instance, going on long nature walks together while sharing new experiences and ideas, cultivating new connections with other couples, taking a yoga or meditation class together, or simply reading the same self-help books (such as this one) and discussing them.

Remember: No employee is an island (or stranded on one, anyway)

"Each life is like a letter of the alphabet. Alone it can be meaningless. Or it can be part of a great meaning."
   — *Anonymous*

We began this little book by talking about the movie "Cast Away," and how the character portrayed by Tom Hanks had managed to shed his corporate identity and uncover his true self after being stranded for many months on a remote and uninhabited island. But while he discovers inner resources he didn't know he possessed, the one thing that he is depicted as being increasingly unable to cope with is his total isolation. So intolerable does he find his solitary existence that, upon discovering a soccer ball among the debris that had floated ashore from his wrecked Fedex plane, he turns it into an imaginary companion—giving it a smiley face and an identity, "Wilson" (the brand name with which the ball is inscribed). For the rest of his time on the island, he regularly converses with Wilson, and when the ball is ultimately lost in the ocean during his attempt to escape, he becomes genuinely grief-stricken.

Like the character in the movie, we all have hidden capabilities, reserves of ingenuity and individual identities that are most often obscured by the disguises, constant demands, and controlling influence of corporate culture. But very few of us could stand to live a totally isolated existence. If for no other reason than to retain our rationality, we must share our lives with others. And that means sharing what we've experienced and whatever we've managed to learn that can help those to whom we relate. Remember: the act of rescuing someone need not necessarily involve a bold act of heroism—it can be as simple as rescuing yourself first, then advising the person how to swim free of a rip tide.

In essence, you can develop all the inner resources it takes to break away from corporate control without having to actually quit your job and risk going broke. But it's not something you should attempt to do alone. You're neither an island nor are you stranded on one—and the process of liberating yourself from the psychological grip of a paycheck is one that should include helping to liberate those around you as well. This is the only way the corporation will eventually become a caring, nurturing structure rather than one that manages people by means of control and fear. By your reading this book and sharing its message with just one person, you have accelerated the process.

Reflections: Exercise 7

Think about someone at work you might mentor—someone newly hired or someone you see as having potential.

_____

What positive attributes does this person possess?

_____

_____

_____

In what areas might you mentor this person?

_____

_____

_____

What might you gain from mentoring this person?

_____

_____

_____

Have you had any mentors in the past? What made them so helpful to you?

_____

_____

_____

Who might you look to as a mentor? What positive qualities does this person possess?

_____

_____

_____

End note

Hopefully, you have begun to implement at least some of the courses of action these seven exercises call for, depending on both your personal inclinations and circumstances. Even if you're not ready for all of them, perhaps you'll wish to go back over one or more at some point in the future. But whichever of these recommendations you choose to follow, seeing them through should empower you to get more enjoyment out of life, feel better, be more motivated, cultivate whatever natural abilities you possess, and most important, escape from the narrow, toxic confines of corporate approval or disapproval that can so easily dominate your existence and affect your self-esteem.

Please e-mail me at Anthony@Detachmentparadox.com and let me know if the exercises contained here have helped you, and, if so, in what ways—along with any other questions or comments you would like to share.

But whatever else you do, just remember—nobody can control you if you refuse to let them.

Footnotes

1. *The McKinsey Quarterly,* 2003, No.2, p.

2. "Health is just steps way,"
   USA Today, Nov. 13, 2002, p. 9D.

3. Reuters, 8/9/03

4. Jerry Useem, From heroes to goats and back again?,
   Fortune, Nov. 18, 2002, pp .41-48.

5. Daniel Vasella, "Temptation is all around us,"
   Fortune, Nov. 18, 2002, pp. 110-112.

6. Stanley Coren, *The Pawprints of History* (The Free Press, 2002),
   pp. 256-258

7. William O. Douglas, *Go East, Young Man:
   The Early Years* (Random House, 1974), p. xii

8. A. Scott Berg, *Goldwyn,* (Alfred A. Knopf, 1989), pp. 9, 407-409.

9. Paul E. McGhee, Ph.D., "Why Companies are Putting Fun to Work,"
   The Laughter Remedy, April, 1999.

10. Terrill Fischer, "Laughter can be cheap cure for workplace ills,"
    Austin Business Journal, 9/29/00.

11. Donna Getzinger, "Good Health is a Laughing Matter: Part
    Two," Sun Integrative Health newsletter, 2001

12. Robert Maurer, Ph.D., "Why Stress Doesn't Exist,"
    Men's Health, September, 2002, pp 96-98.

13. Robert G. Allen, The Importance of Mentorship,
    EmpowerMag.com

14. Ibid